Stay Human

Poetry and Prose

June Barefield

inner child press, ltd.

'building bridges of cultural understanding'

Credits

Author
June Barefield

Editor
hülya n. yılmaz, Ph.D.

Cover Designer
inner child press international

Book Designer
William S. Peters, Sr.

Publisher
inner child press international

General Information

Stay Human

June Barefield

1st Edition: 2025

This publication is protected under the Copyright Law as a "Collection." All rights for all submissions are retained by the individual author and/or artist. No part of this publishing may be reproduced or transferred in any manner without the prior **WRITTEN CONSENT** of the "Material Owner" or its representative, Inner Child Press. Any such violation infringes upon the Creative and Intellectual Property of the Owner, pursuant to International and Federal Copyright Law. Any queries pertaining to this "Collection" should be addressed to the Publisher of Record.

Publisher Information

Inner Child Press:
www.innerchildpress.com

This Collection is protected under U.S. and International Copyright Laws.

Copyright © 2025: June Barefield

ISBN-13: 978-1-961498-63-1 (inner child press, ltd.)

Price: $ 25.95

Disclaimer

During the evaluation and editing process, we have found it necessary to leave certain selective passages, diction, punctuation, specific use of CAPS, bolding, and colloquialisms intact. We strongly feel that the unique elements of June Barefield's creative expressions yield a finitely authentic reading experience. Our goal is to honor and maintain the author's undisputed voice.

hülya n. yılmaz, Ph.D.
Director of the Department of Editing Services
Inner Child Press International

"All people dream, but not equally. Those who dream at night in the dusty recesses of their minds wake in the day to find that it was vanity. But the dreamers of the day are dangerous people, for they may act their dream with open eyes to make it possible." ~ T.E. Lawrence

Eva, you are a huge part of the reason I am able to dream at all. I am so grateful to call you sister, and to have you up to this very day in my corner. You have always been there, available, no matter the situation or circumstances. Like a backstop for whenever I missed a pitch. I never had to run far to retrieve the ball and get back into the game. I know you have prayed for me, worried for me, and even attempted to advise me, admonishing me in a way no one else would dare. I love you for eternity, Eva Marie. Thank you for caring for me. This collection of thoughts, *Stay Human,* I dedicate to you.

Table of Contents

Preface   *xiii*

The Prose and the Poetry

Understand This	3
The 'Afro-American Negro'	4
Without Eyes	8
Sometimes	10
Educational Programming, the System, and the Machine	13
Burn It Down	16
Labor	18
shade	19
Babel	21
Pieces	22
Career	24
Sects and Prisms, and Systems and Shit	25
All Alone Again	27
Oasis	29
Bad Magic	30
The City	34
Anything	36
Lantern	37
Down Here	39
A Dream	40
Unhappy Savage	41
A Time to Kill	42
Turn It Off!	43

Table of Contents ... continued

Media	45
Her	46
Not Forever	47
i see	48
Beethoven	50
Earth, Moon & Pyramid	51
Season	52
I Know	53
Men Must Act	55
New Illusion	58
Kingly Conception	59
Little Man	62
4NOW	64
Eugenics. The End Game: Population Control	66
. . . But Apart	68
Ruin	70
Define Freedom	71
My Urban Analysis	73
Culture & Law	75
No Us	76
Help Me!	78
TOMB	80
War	81
Look Outside	83
My Good Friend Insomnia	85
Gravity	86
Master	87
A Nigga	89

Table of Contents ...continued

All Men	90
I Think	92
Climate Change: The Global Warming Swindle	94
Insomnia	97
Photograph	100
Selah	103
936	104
KaLeB Flow	105
Professional Negro	106
A Longing	107
Life Dance	108
Citizen	109
Fish	111
Upside-down	113
Demon	114
Another Un-poetiK **Rant**!	116
Human Animal	120
The Future	121
Endemic	123
Negrotudes	124
2099	125
How?	126
Namesake	127
Bourgeoisie Negro	129
Wind	132
No Reprieve	134
Who Is "They"?	135
Dark Matter	136

Table of Contents ... continued

Premonition	138
Infected	140
A Witness	141
The Only "Why"	143
Xposed	144
Sickness	146
Ice Cream	148
Faustian Bargain	150
Beautiful SouL	152
Is-ness	153
Another Now	155
Antithesis	156
Presence	157
Conflagration Destination	158
Eclipse	160
Void	162
liar	164
No Respite	165
ameriKa	167
Free at Last	169
Turn	170
Imagine	172
Open Streets	173
Shadow	176
Haze	177
Ideation	179
Façade	180
Bang!	182

Table of Contents ... continued

Misremember?	185
We Die	187
Passover	189
Who Will Do?	191
This Night	194
bird	195
Swan	196
Question Mark Missing	197
Progress	199
Asylum	200
Destiny	203
ameriKan me	204
Thought Babel	206
Unreasonable, Always	209
Forget Not	211
What Them Say	213
Never Tell	214
A Propositional Plea	217
Smile	219
Contrast Defined	220
For the Unwashed Masses	223
Hourglass	225
Negro Telepathy	227
FLASHbacK	228
Panic	229
Omitting eYe	230
Half	231
2 Save the World	234

Table of Contents ... continued

ID	236
The First Virtue	238
The World	239
On Purpose	241
Comparably	243
Human ChiKens	244
Hate Speech	245
The Falcon	247
Babylon	248
Her Eyes	249
Promise	250
United We Stand	251
Every Star	252
Dreamy Enough	253
Anarchy Now	256
Now, Here We All Are	257
Rules for Being Human	260
Stay Human	261

Epilogue

A Few Words from the Author	265
The Author's Afterword	267
Acknowledgements	275
Glossary Notes	277
References	281
Other Works by the Author	283

Preface

In this material world in which we live, what part does the human being play in his or her own existence? Is perception reality? And if it is not reality, who controls perception, and how?

Considering what the world is now, with all of the conflicts and misery, the destructive brutality, and violence, man is still as he has always been. He remains callously competitive, acquisitive, and a narcissist; so, of course, the system which he has built around him is as he is. And what he is, I am, or certainly have been, a creature of materialism and mindless consumption, too well-adjusted to a sick society. Acculturated into a series of institutions, be they political, legal, religious, monetary; to institutions of familial values, social class, and occupational specialty. These are the places and structures that influence and shape understanding and create the perspective in which reality is interpreted.

Incrementally, society has been formulated to control thinking. Nothing is natural, and the so-called citizen knows not self-reliance, but only conformity. The government is God, and money is The Lord. We're born ignorant to ignorant parents in a society that's ignorant; so, ignorance is the norm. Indoctrination, we call "education," hypnotism, "entertainment"; we refer to criminals as our leaders, and we "believe" that the lie is truth because our collective mind has never really been our own.

Our thoughts are like driftwood; society is the river, flowing always into the ocean, but we know not the moon. We are out of rhythm, off balance, and out of sync with nature. The very reason we do not know that we've been lied to, conditioned, and brainwashed is because we have been lied to, conditioned, and brainwashed! My identity itself has been prepackaged for me; so was my daddy's, and his before him. Prepackaged at different levels for different reasons at different times.

A blind man's bluff is this game of compliance, and the pathology of the rich is whom and what we serve. For my entire life, I've recklessly wondered why all of this is, pondering who I am, and what the reason is for this madness.

And I believed, attempting to make the world less complicated, gazing intently through the skewed lenses I'd formulated for myself simply by being alive, a slave to my emotions and the opinions of others. Unknowingly, we take the way from man; from our parents, teachers, coaches, peer groups, and we adapt to our environment accordingly, thinking thoughts manufactured by the machine, believing.

There's a quote by Langston Hughes where he says, "When you turn the corner and run into yourself, then you know that you have turned all of the corners that are left." This is that. This is me, coming to a place in life and realizing that it was me. I am the world, and all of my observations of the world and its madness are observations of me. This book is, strangely enough, at its core, the long process of my individual attempt at change. *Stay Human* is me searching for my soul. It was written in various places in America. It was written while I battled with myself about the meaning of life, mostly straddling the fence with at least two or three toes still in the streets. A double-minded man, me, is unstable in all that he does. *Stay Human* is harsh and judgmental, and even vicious in spots. I decided to put it out while attempting to write a book dedicated to my mother about beautiful things. The poem "Stay Human" actually being the first of such writings for her book. I'm obviously not quite ready, shall we say, to being beautiful for an entire book. Not yet! I'd like to think, like Assata said, "I must confess that waltzes do not move me. I have no sympathy for symphonies. I guess I hummed the Blues too early, and spent too many midnights out wailing to the rain."

All of the vitriol contained herein, I assure you, is simply an observation of myself in the world. I didn't write this for anyone. These words are part of me in an attempt to exorcise the monsters of my thought patterns. I am, as I often tell my friends, in the 4th quarter of my life, and *Stay Human* was written so that my children can look at this years from now, and consider truth, falsehood, integrity, and hope. I want them to "know", you know? Everything must come to pass in its proper time and place. In the meantime, please, *Stay Human*.

Stay Human

Poetry and Prose

June Barefield

Stay Human

"In a decaying society, art, if it is truthful, must also reflect decay. And unless it wants to break faith with its social function, art must show the world as changeable. And help to change it."

Ernst Fischer (1899-1972)

Austrian journalist, writer, and politician

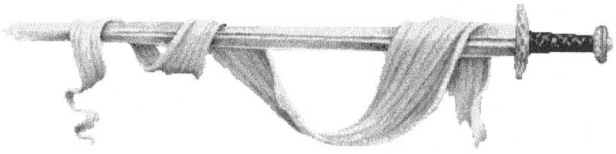

June Barefield

Understand This

In pursuit of that beautiful soul within
The universe of SELF
Where the past is read
And the future is **RED**
Where only omens and outlaws may tread
And everyday is also NIGHT on the horizons of life
And men are all of mice
And versa vice
Through every sufferance, and all of the pain
Deep down inside where breath rests
Just left of RIGHT, back behind your chest plate, surrounded by ribs
Where harmony and silence provide the answers on this quest
And truth's alive, attracting life thru' the eyes
PURIFIED 7 TIMES
Penetrating
Powerful
Protected & Present
In love, like seas and sands on distant shores,
     whispering a song, beautifully exquisite, like a summer's breeze
Where I am that He is, one must explore to B peAce
And the only real risky bet is regret
And the only REAL message needed
     can only be provided exactly where you are at.

UNDERSTAND THIS.

Stay Human

The 'Afro-American Negro'

Perhaps what the oppressed masses of "black" people need today is some sort of missive from another age. A magical message in a time capsule, somehow preserved by the ancestors. A fiery, impetuous outburst of defiance, determination, will, and self-mastery. But perhaps that may only be realized in a 'Holly Weird' production, so we can all have a proper dream to distract us all from reality. I heard Cornell "Cornball" West in an interview claim that "Empire must be critiqued, and critiqued with integrity." and that what we're experiencing today in ameri**K**a amongst ourselves is what he called, "ruthless ambition by the lumpen bourgeois."

Cornball is a fancy nigga, ain't he? I agree with the good Dr. West, but who the fuck am I to disagree with him. After all, he's "the expert," a pedagogue, and nation-builder, a superb communicator, and "educated." So clever is he that he and others of his particular ilk are ever aware of who it is that butters their proverbial brisket. The negro would never fix his mouth to call out his subsidizers.

I believe that with no other goal in mind but to be the beneficiaries of the decadent institutions that separate, distract, confuse, and ultimately coalesce into a process of thought, ripe with chaos and confusion, is the reason that this upper crust American Negro is allowed to exist. They let us call it 'black excellence'! And we, together, all **believe**! We idolize and hold up into the air above us, what should be torn down with extreme prejudice. In my humble opinion, what it really is, is what it's always been, only in a different suit and tie. An entertaining con job, a calculated fraud. I also believe that these particular Dr. Cornell West types began their journey with pure intent.

If you'd like to know about the design of intention, read Screwtape's assertion given to his underling demon Wormwood in CS Lewis' classic, *The Screwtape Letters*.

Meanwhile, as the great masses of The Negro Afro-Ameri**K**an People are effectively being entertained, the attack dog police are more than willing to murder us in the street. I think at the very root and core of black-white relations in ameri**K**a is the story of the Afri**K**an enslavement. The story of the white free man and the black slave. This pathology remains "Willie Lynch," and through this centuries-old strategy of psychological, historical, and social oppression to tame the negro, the white man has secured his manhood, his dominance and control.

June Barefield

Today, in what's left of what they'd like for you and me to "believe" is Contemporary Black America, is, as far as I can tell, mostly disillusionment.

The so-called 'Black middle class' has become, as Dr. Cornball put it, "well-adjusted to injustice and well-adapted to indifference," comfortable and ignorant. But the comfort part is coming to an end. Dare I point out just briefly the black professional class, the black political class, following its pied piper, Mr. Barry Hussein Obama, with all of his paternalistic, symbolic rhetoric, neoliberal, pro-drone, pro-massive surveillance, pro-**Palestine** occupation, pro-ecological devastation, and pro-massive incarceration . . . they (we) just follow along, never missing a note, or ever taking his record to task?

"If you want to hide something from a nigga, just put it in a book!" The facts of your illustrious pied piper, Mr. Barry Hussein Obama, have all been written down, but that ignorant mainstream negro here in our fair ameri**K**a still stands up proud and tall in defiance, over that old "Change you can believe in" garbage! The masses of the people are always seduced by mere window dressing, smoke and mirrors, the proverbial carrot on a stick, held just out of reach by the Negro technocrat, continuing to "lead" us directly or indirectly into and out of this chasm where we are told we are free. Refusing to see that freedom in the USA is just code for slavery. I think "they" call it **cognitive dissonance**. Comparatively, among the Black masses of people resides a desperation so deep, a hunger so acute, that this external imperialism, the shit show of the so-called progressive politics, funded corporately, is accepted; somehow, even longed for.

In this country, I believe that authority is too often simply a cover for wrong. We've got volumes upon volumes of literature in reference to what I'll term our collective "love warriors," the Ida B. Wells, the Ella Bakers, and our beloved Dr. Martin Luther King, Jr., but respectfully, I do not believe that today, the masses of people (Black people) have the luxury of a non-violent struggle; if, indeed, there's any **struggle** left in us. To forgive one's oppressors over and again in this climate where citizens are being systematically gunned down in a murderous frenzy, is foolish cowardice. Forgiveness in relation to the ongoing, all-encompassing oppression of the poor and working class Black people in this nation. How does it remain a viable option in the hearts and minds of the masses? It's almost as if Black people in ameri**K**a are under some sort of wicked spell, in a trance that cannot be broken, not until it is broken, and it must be broken. "Revolution is not a fruit that falls because it is ripe, we must make it fall," as the legendary, the honorable Che Guevara put it back when these illicit freedom boundaries were being shattered and replaced with self-determination and the revolutionary zeal of gods!

Stay Human

The so-called Negro in ameri**K**a has been taken through so many different stages of slavery, domination, colonization, degradation, repression, and murder, that it's a wonder he still even exists! The great and all powerful eugenics lobby has been hard at work on the problem of our **existence** for some time now, though. Personally, I don't think a beautiful weed can be exterminated, but annihilation is at hand nevertheless. This is, was, has been, and will forever remain 'THE Plan' for the so-called ameri**K**an negro. And still, what we look to do is laud the very entity that has subjugated the masses of us here in this place called "America".

I think forgiveness is the highest form of love. Black people can collectively love all people, as any tribe of humans should. In my everyday life and experience, from my own personal serfdom in this nation, whom the Black man and woman love especially is their Caucasian benefactor. We are still today, in 2025, attempting to rearrange the Master's House by using the Master's Tools. That my friend is pathological. I've seen it over and again, a sickness exists within the diaspora of my people at the spiritual level. While our individual as well as our collective self-hate abounds, what we have been cleverly trained to do is to turn the other cheek, look the other way, and live inside the structures of White Racist Supremacy. Any talk of forgiveness and a non-violent "protest" is just a special kind of gibberish about Black people remaining calm and serene, deferential, and unwilling to straighten up our backbones to fight. "There can be no forgiveness of the oppressor while the oppressor is engaged in oppression." Another Cornball West quote! One of the many Black intellectual types that Charlie keeps on the conveyor belt at the Higher Learning factories across this nation. The crisis of the so-called Black intellectual is a crisis of consciousness. From my vantage point, down here on the main street with the chikens, what I've become sadly aware of is just tokenism. An Uncle Tom competition, a comparison narrative for the hearts and minds of the people.

The government raises up and stamps the peppercorned token, negro, in its Institutions for Higher Learning to keep the masses of Black people at bay. And we worship them!

There's a terrifying sort of moral apathy, a death of the heart and spirit, a very strong delusion that we're under. It's propagated for a reason in these factories for the 'Greek Negro' to be trained and grow rich. Objective morality is disappearing at the same time as a billion of ameri**K**a's buried Black corpses are beginning to speak. I hear them all calling out from their graves, still begging to be free! Do you hear them? Can you not see? The animal heads of our Ancient gods are returning, and the wake of oblivion has dawned.

June Barefield

The shortsighted, ignorant mass of Afro-American Negro sheep, like me, the peasant class, motivated by envy, and so easily fooled? **Selah**. From this moment forward, despair ends and tactics begin.

God will not have Her work made manifest by cowards. **Men must act**.

Without Eyes

For some of us, a crust of bread
To others, a Lamborghini

I get it, crocodiles weep
Deep, like elevator music,
    played while hallucinating about a dream
Without eyes
Ears
Nose
Or throat
Where the sheep and the goat, both float away into the
    ethereal aesthetic
Surrounded by man's inventions

New men
Made of computer applications
And identity existence
Peace programs
And pharmaceutical conventions
Moving in syncopation with the diagram
All replaceable
Flying heavenward through the eye of a needle
    with firecrackers up their asses
Clients of the institution
Constituents of the delusion

I get it tho', crocodiles weep
Without eyes
Ears
Nose
Or throat
The sheep and the goat, together
Insinuating every deviation of time
In line, impatiently waiting
Both deathly afraid of suffocating
Obsessing over the logic in the lie

June Barefield

The desperation of the crimes
The despondency of the mind
Easing starward in an iodine drift
Oozing eastward with the mud tides

Without eyes.

Stay Human

Sometimes

Sometimes we think maybe no Dragons remain
That all the Nobles have gone
Yet, somehow, we feel safe
Content inside this semi-conscious mind-state
Together but apart
Wide awake but asleep
Inside the herd, out of danger
Agreeably estranged from peace
But sooner or later
We turn into exactly what we are pretending to be
Shrinking slowly
Fading
Mind's eYe closing
Glimmering, but dimly. from time to time
Up until time exposes the ultimate tale
A twisted duality dialogue
Transfixed to a 4sale sign dichotomy
Unsure and afraid
Waning
Thinking no Dragons remain
That all the Nobles have left
Hidden inside the herd
Pretending conventional wisdom holds the license
A warrant guaranteeing your very soul and breath
Sometimes
We swallow up all of the mercury

Gradually, asphyxiation takes hold
While we bob and weave up the avenue of moments, incomplete
Mind-controlled
Where the gentle, safe, popular, easy slope is our only hope
Or so it seems
But sooner or later
Sometimes
All you'll ever be, even in the center of the middle, is lukewarm
Where "all is a riddle, and the key to the riddle, another riddle . . ."

June Barefield

The reason perhaps no Dragons remain
Why all the Nobles have gone

Sometimes.

Stay Human

"The aim of public education is not to spread enlightenment at all; it is simply to reduce as many individuals as possible to the same safe level, to breed and train a standardized citizenry, to put down dissent and originality. That is its aim in the United States, whatever the pretensions of politicians, pedagogues, and other such mountebanks, and that is its aim everywhere else."

Henry Louis Mencken (1880-1956)

American journalist, essayist, satirist, and cultural critic

June Barefield

Educational Programming, the System, and the Machine

Your life is a lie. From the moment you could walk, they've been programming your mind. And this mind is we, in the aggregate, because you are me, and shit, collectively we never stood a chance. We were open, trusting, curious, and "they" knew it! This is how they do it, stepping in before thinking for yourself is possible.

Your parents could never stop it from happening to you. Hell, it happened to them first! Caught up in the same systematic rendering designed to shape and control human beings. Nobody asked for this programming, but here we all are, carrying this weight, feeling as if something is missing, like your life isn't fully your own. It's classical conditioning to keep us safe and turn us into productive members of a society insane. Makes you wonder if there's such a thing as out-sane?

Follow me now . . .

These systems, education, media, politi**K**, religion, entertainment, and even the "food" we consume, were not made available for anyone to prosper from. They were built to keep you compliant, small, and predictable. A deliberate system of control. For control. Control over you and what you feel, know, desire, what you hope for . . . For control. From the first bell you heard at school to the television, and all the little gadgets created that enable you and me to think only the thoughts manufactured for us by this machine for control.

What the all-knowing, "they" do not want you to know is that you have the tools and the power inside of you to break away from the meat puppet game and reclaim your own brain. They don't want anyone to think critically, not for themselves. They want for the masses, they need the masses of the people, to just follow their rules, buy up their products, pay your fucking taxes, and stay within the lines of the boundaries drawn out for you. This is how to "educate" a fool and keep the status quo intact, operating as efficiently and officially as possible. They've been making slaves for generations at different levels, in different times, for different reasons. We're taught obedience so seamlessly from generation to generation that we don't even realize what's being done to us. Society wasn't designed to nurture individuality, but suppress it, and keep you predictably predictable, and easy to control.

Under the guise of education, they have made the individual human being from one generation to the next merely products. We've been shaped into compliant participants in the machinery of placation and subordination until death. They want you in debt, tied to their financial systems forever, until death. And then? Your children may live just as you did, tied to a wage, a slave. A polite, well-behaved, contrite little system clowns, and you'd best behave. It's no wonder to anyone who's thinking just a little bit that the prisons mirror the schools. Both receive their monies based on numbers alone. They need to fill the classrooms/prison cells with fresh bodies to receive government funds. In either predicament, the monies spent never benefit any human being, not really. Schools shape obedient workers, and prisons manage those who step out of line.

Stay Human

Lines drawn for the compliant mind to mime. One coin, two sides, equals profit for shaping, and the formation of an obedient mankind. All of this for profit alone.

They don't give a fuck about us. The foundation of this lifelong programming starts, of course, in childhood. The systems that claim to educate you are not only teaching, they are conditioning you as well. You're trained to follow rules, respect authority, and suppress your individual self. All of this is done under the guise of learning. Education is what they call it, but it's always been about control. There's no space anywhere in the classroom for independence of thought. School is a factory of conformist molding and shaping the young into the same trap. Education is not designed to empower anyone, rather to mold you into a predictable, compliant cog in the machine. You must become predictable because that's what enables control to thrive.

The system wants only that you submit. All the talk about being independent and "free" is the bullshit contrived from the collective compliant mind. Call it doublespeak or whatever you wish. In a system built on obedience, independent thought is taken as a threat. It's always safest for the individual sheep when he or she is comfortable inside of the herd. Uniform and normalized is best. Speaking of which, standardized tests aren't a measure of intelligence at all. They're a measure of obedience for all the little robot children who got all the shiny bright blue stars on their report cards! For those "students most adept at remaining inside the lines provided them by the state, congratulations! For the tiny matter of innovation, creativity, or critical thinking? None of that will ever be welcome into a system, the system, our system, that runs on the notion that you will comply. Nobody wants anybody thinking differently. Everybody wants both nobody and anybody to fit the mold, follow the script, and to never ask questions that are outside of the lines. That means everybody!

School for the majority of people only prepares you for a lifetime of mediocrity. It feeds envy and jealousy, breeds ignorant competition, and ties a person's self-worth to a dollar bill and the approval of others. Fuck school!

Remember Pavlov's experiment where he rang a bell, and the dogs began to salivate, expecting food. Over time, they could care less about the food, all they wanted was to hear that bell. The schoolhouse is full of Pavlov's dogs, ain't it? The bell rings, and our automatic, trained response is to obey without questioning. Educated to follow orders, schooled to comply. The reason many of these little boys and girls, myself included, grow up and join the military service or become police officers is to follow orders. The orders do not have to be morally upright. Any order issued by an authority will be followed regardless, and human beings are slaughtered. If we need to place any blame at all, then it is the order follower at fault for every atrocity, large or small.

We do not realize that "just doing your job" enables the controllers to control. Schools manufacture thousands of these idiots every year after graduation! Useful enough, trained up just enough to serve and follow orders. The most powerful lessons in school are the ones you aren't aware you're learning. Unaware, we learn to like to obey authority. Submission is the ultimate lesson of life. To submit. To fear failure because mistakes are to be punishable. To seek validation. All of the gold stars and "good" grades condition children to value external approval over their own instincts and intuitions, making them easy to manipulate.

The education system sets the foundation for all the other programming to come in and capture your thinking. The lessons of conformity are reinforced through the media and entertainment we ingest into what would be our individual desires and dreams. Whatever you consume is what ultimately shapes who it is you will become. To instill Right Knowledge, together, we must teach our children the truth. We must unlock their brains and never repeat the lies of yesterday. We cannot feed our babies the same lies we ate; otherwise, who will they become? If we don't teach them, who will? A school? Who will they become, you? What will they do, grow up and work? Why?

They've been making slaves for generations.

We're in a strange place right now in the world. To me, it seems that "we" are finding more and more a sort of cruel enjoyment in our servitude.

The mind of a child is where the Revolution begins. The condition of the comfortable slave must end.

Let it be,
. . . and so it is
WE MUST TEACH THEM.

Stay Human

Burn It Down

Hidden in their asphalt jungles
Levied with 9-5 type sorrows
Or locked up in their dungeons
This, your experience
Your environment
Every directive
All instruction
For a stock profit
On a kourt docket
Nary a nickel out of pocket
A nigga, just a drop in a wealthy white man's bucket
The assimilation covet is no conundrum
Them call it "education"
Where every decree, pertaining to the so-called ameri**K**an negro
Every ingredient for this recipe to keep men impoverished
Written out of the life equation
Systematically demolished
Locked down or wasting away on the corporate plantation
To placate an entire Nation of Black men
A process properly preparing men to be institute property
By design
I see you smiling with tolerance tho'
Ignorant to the ameri**K**an dream
Asleep; so, a part of you "believes"
Shit, nightmares are dreams too, but who has time to dream?
It's hard enough try'na figure out when next you might eat, where you might sleep

Seems to be that the so-called negro has been bought and sold for too cheap!
They've raised up a talented ten percent in order to perpetrate their cultural
    con game scheme
Creating shepherds from amongst the sheep
And for these,
There must be No Reprieves!

But for the bringers of darkness
To those that own their thoughts
Those that struggle
For the Star and the Atom, transmitted into matter
As black and as pale as the circumstance that you remain under
Numb 2 what them say matters

June Barefield

Aware of "the lie"
Consider for a moment this humming machine of light
A determination of grace in time
Where truth survives for every survivor
Naturally selected to be sacrificed
The dancers of the NOW must be willing to sacrifice, and struggle
Together
Flout the transgressor
Fuck the oppressor
DISOBEY!
Right now
Do not allow yourself to remain hidden inside their asphalt jungle carousels,
    backs against the wall, enraged
For the bringers of darkness
Beautiful & righteous

Allow not cameras for the Hunger Game Managers
For the love of liberty
For human dignity
Dancers of the now
Straighten up your backbones and stand up
Now
Struggle together again, Now
Break every chain
Organize Worldwide
DEFINE DEFIANCE
Disobey!!
Light the fucking match
Dancers of the now
To the bringers of darkness
BURN IT DOWN.

Stay Human

Labor

In the people's centuries-long struggle for the liberties promised and promulgated so eloquently in the Bill of Rights, industrial feudalism has remained steadfast. Certainly, it's morphed and changed in name and title, but ultimately, even today, a peasant is a peasant and a lord is still a noble, a controller. In a combination of legal, economic, military, cultural, and political systems broadly defined to structure society from generation to generation, so it remains.

Terrorism is still inflicted by hired gunmen, today referred to as "police." In an American Labor History Theme Study, I read a quote from a Railroad Labor Boss that boasted, "I can hire one half of the working class to kill the other half!" Competition amongst the peasant class is paramount in the maintenance and control of said peasant. The poor, working class people are truly a kin to livestock. The reality of the consumer class is slavery, and the unreality is the appearance that men and women in ameriKa are tied to and part of the mechanisms of control over their lives.

This thinking is laughable.

A very beloved, wealthy fellow, by the name of Sir James Madison made it abundantly clear, stating that, "power should always be in the hands of the rich." By contrast, the elite members of an insane society not only have all the "money" but they also own and create every opportunity to get more. All the knowledge and all the power in every so-called civilized nation is a model for class conflict. Your beloved Sir James Madison knew very well that the agrarian American Dream of your other beloved rich fella, Sir Thomas Jefferson, would not be replicated in the 19th century. Industrial Kapitalism has devoured and displaced even the idea of any democratic republiK of relatively "equal" people, equal white people, of course. The 20th century has come and gone, building along with it an insidiously hideous distribution of wealth and the incumbent power.

The future is here! In the 25th year of the 21st century, first month, 20th day, now you's a nigga too! How does it feel?

shade

in the land of shade trees
everything is good
it's easy to remember
golden rules
in golden days
even "God" is good
underneath the shade
amazing dreams of peacocks
and television violence
pervading sensational ism's
a cultural hypnosis
creating a mass psychosocial benign alliance
comfortable and warm
totally compliant
underneath your shade trees
holding your breath
praying over rosary beads
easy to mold, cut, compress, and fold
with the golden rules
in golden days
watching the grass grow in the shade
but across the landscape
carved up in the city
there's no progress to profess
no open sky
a process
the disorganized urbanite
him, circadian cycle a conflict of confusion undressed
and peaceful visions die
in the fragmented testimony
of a weak alibi
in context
the money gods have taken over the mass mind
peace creeps cry out to polluted skies
sunlight reflects from broken mirror shards
Amun **RA** light
no trinity headline is worthy now
green-eyed Egyptian alley cat cry out when the moon **rise**

Stay Human

from time thru' time to time anon
vaulted from place to place over oblivion
and in the east white sunlight,
professional suburbanites arrive each morning with brief-cased minds
in suit and tie, perpetuating the lie
with smiling eyes
b4 the moonrise, them wave goodbye
back to suburbia
where the shade trees line up for lunch
flowers are within reach and quiet hands touch
in the land of golden rules
for golden days
on shaded lawns
where you're told it's safe
the syphilis of the congenial live out this lust
civil virtue,
like paint that persists on rusted tin,
fighting this everyday war of the mass routine
suburban tranquility
merely afterthoughts of institutions made greater than our rage
fed twinkies and television, dreaming of the lottery sweepstakes
every whisper, wandering slowly concealing the grave
it's easy to remember golden rules
in golden days
even "GOD" is good
underneath the shade.

Babel

In our comfort,
We have forgotten the forgotten
The unbegun begotten,
Wrapped up together comfortably in the King's cotton
Whatever that initial ember was, we cannot remember
Reaping only fruit as it rottens
A lifetime of winter
We've disavowed into the aether
Disconnected from this memory
"i am that He is"
In our comfort, only convenience will appease us now
We have forgotten
"The nameless ones who came before, but are no more"
Somewhere, somehow, in our comfort,
We've turned cold
We've forgotten to remember that this comfort in actuality, the completion of image,
A mine mold, cemented now in ignorance
To ignore this generational darkness
Imagine now Mastery without your master's impedance
The question without answers, hence, an answer-less equation
12 tribes One Nation
We have forgotten our own enslavement
Prince Hall, the pimp perfecting this derangement,
Pandering amongst the people to create for himself a new arrangement
Forgetting
It's Hunger games for the poor
Disavowed into the aether
Disconnected from this memory
In our comfort,
The entire Western Collective,
Eating the bread, watching the circus, playing the life game on knees and hand
Bowing low at the altar of acceptance
To be accepted, regardless of the bloodletting
And this is humanity in "The West"
The comfortable collective
Forgetting the forgotten.

Stay Human

Pieces

Learned lots of lessons living life afraid to ask any questions
Second-guessing what folk are taught to "believe" is fact
Disengage do I completely from the **culture** TRAP
Looking back this apprehension, my sole protection
Now I collect precious nuggets of truth
Strip mined the depths of me to separate the dross from the jewels
Inside this fiery furnace, the absolute
Where Mother is Nature and Her Law remains the glue
Understanding kindness, finally realizing the inheritance of a fool
A very cruel reality to swallow, digest, and extract from my pattern of thought
INTROSPECTIVE reflections, too congested 2 see through
Watching the sellout show,
Waiting for a cue
It's true, under the sun, there is absolutely nothing new
And 4 my Dearly Departed,
A confirmation of this fear I erase
Facing myself alone
I so miss you
Because I AM you
The love, the joy,
And the pieces of you at peace with you
. . . But then
Again this fear
Like an estate plan for man's completion
A bequest, signifying every institution
Where citizens are patients, infected with the virus of a conformity existence
Some type of bourgeois dream deferred,
Supposing that from here on out everything will be beautiful
& wonderful
Increasingly exquisite
& marvelous
Thinking it likely that "heaven" awaits with golden streets and pearly gates
I "believe" there's a poem somewhere, perhaps on the bottom of the ocean's floor,
Wrapped up snugly, this ballad, along with the keys to the Kingdom
The questions, questioning always the present,
"Knowing" the past,
Believing only upon today
Understanding that "soul work" is but serendipity and simplicity,
Dipped in what's real
Awareness made clear

June Barefield

Right here
4 the right now
Today
From centuries of a patient sentiment,
Lacing together the winds and tides, gods and earths, the moons and planets
All particles of this electric river flow, raught to be harnessed
Brought into being out of darkness
In the beginning, foundationally fortified
Never to be undermined or subverted, sabotaged, or threatened
Nature's law B not suggestive or arbitrary or ever morally relative
Made from the molten masses, cooled underneath depths unknown
This is where *stillness* is embraced
Inside of you
A single door leading into a temple few consider anymore
For the love, the joy,
and the pieces of you at peace with you
Yet, still, eYe question
So many lessons filled with blank spaces and unrealized confessions
Masking kindness to embrace counterfeit intentions,
Cursed with the blessing sanctioned by pretension,
Addressing life's sojourn, honing in on the present
Indecision, a decision
An ongoing quest to understand the essence
A soul work soliloquy
Serendipity from simplicity
The questions
The complicity
And this *fear*
To face one's **self** alone
For the love
For the joy
For all of the pieces of you at peace with you.

Career

To want more than anything
And give up everything to get it
But then, after you get it
You realize that it's not that great after all
You realize that you have no life
No life that's your own
Career,
Life, owned
Even your thoughts
Paid for, purchased, and sold
A 20th century invention
All pretension
For the overly competitive
The ambitious
For comparison
An inheritance
A pathological condition
Career
Over everything.

June Barefield

Sects and Prisms, and Systems and Shit

A relatively irrelevant ism, rearranging new schisms from start to finish
From prism to prison back to the privilege of living
Only to enter a brand new prism
To "think"
Free of the contemporary conceptualization of any system
An earthbound journey
Continuum
Underneath the wing of the dragon
In a world system
An open-air prison
Red pill dilemma
Blue pill distraction
Division
Distortion
A warped inversion
Civilized divergence
Antennas up, plugged into self-satisfaction
An excursion,
Distracted by the rhetorical
Redacted and redefined,
Undermined and made historical
So negros everywhere rock the vote!
But Master selects just whom to promote
Unwilling to embrace the despicable truth of the lie
Twisted and animalistic
Conceptualized systems
Contemporary victims
Sadistic and vile
Political actors make millions
Civilians celebrate them and impersonate the lie
Chameleons,
The minions participate
Citizen complicit, "Thinking" with a crocodile's mind
About:
"A change you can believe in"
While what **destruction** truly means is:
"Building something back better"
Call it "Newspeak"
And of course:
To "Make ameri**K**a WHITE (great) again"

Stay Human

And so, the un-begun begin again
Cycled in and out of make-believe, in the name of democracy
The people participate and the complicity is in the compromise
And we, the people, have all been
Compromised
So, maybe it's time to shake the dead awake?
Erase the detestable credibility of the lie,
Define defiance, simply
DO NOT COMPLY.

June Barefield

All Alone Again

Another strange city
Always, in actuality, practically every city is the same city
Where casually, city after city, we pity the unpretty
So **I observe**:
Pretentiousness and preoccupation are the typical narratives, where most all have silly
Little marriages with their telecommunications devices, dulled and diluted, dumbed
    down,
Without attentiveness, pulling narcissistic, little, miniature poodles, in fancy little
Carriages
Strangely the same in every single city

Our inter-connectivity, an unreliable reality
And integrity has been genetically modified

The people are just patients, patented miserably for middle-class failure
Merely mules,
Beasts of burden,
Buried alive inside a paradoxical, perfumed, unadvertised, day time drama,
Made for TV with faulty pressure systems, being transmission-belted into the oblivion
Of the mundane,
Moving in and out of our comfort stations, vacant
. . . ***Just waiting***
And nothing but money is sacred
Naked, little, ignoble rats gnawing on existence without any iron at all left in the phallus
Soft and off-balance,
Callous inside, bouncing on a soap bubble up the avenue of someone else's time,
Seemingly at ease, always waiting in another line
BLIND.
Kindness is worn like a disguise by the meek, for the mild, all the crocodiles' men remain
Beguiled
. . . ***meantime***

Somewhere down in the sewers of existence, they cook up the cancers with a smile
And transparent parrots conspire to inherit some iron cage, carried like a ball and chain
By your parents
Intolerant, penny-pinching wenches
String-saving, petty-bourgeois, an invisible hand seizing the larynx; at which, rosy little
Crucifixes dangle dutifully around the neck of the incoherent
Saturated completely now

Stay Human

Wet through and filled up with the indiscriminate, wholesale wish-dom
Of this world's nonsense
Another strangely familiar city,
Unproductively out of focus
I observe, and so, I am all alone again.

June Barefield

Oasis

In my mind's eYe, I am walking towards a great, distant tower atop a majestic mountain somewhere *far away from here,* into the future regions of time and space. In my mind, it is beautiful. I have the vision of a hawk, the hearing of a doe, all of my senses are vigorously alive. I slowly stride into, and then, out of time and equation. *I am present*, surveying everything all at once with such simplicity. In my mind, I am alive, and it is so beautiful. In my mind, an Oasis.

Bad Magic

A genetic echo, recollection, trance
A memory dance, ignored
Absent of mind, inattentive to earth
Every inheritance, coerced
Rehearsed, neglect
The curse
Never to be forgotten

Every living thing stalked by the predatorial
All prey, praying to be the predator one day
With god
In death masks, preying
Concealing genuine essence
Essentially, the absence of progression
Preying with god
Fugitive feelings become useless contention
Fugitive futures capitulate to the captured
An obsession
Pretending
In death masks, making contrition
New faces tell old lies and cross the rubicon
Disguised
Cold alibis contrive
Raged ones now rise because hurt cannot hurt anymore
A compromised existence for life
Hurt alone endure the absent of mind
And for what?
Why?

New faces, old lies, the Bad Magic demise

Every aggression, justified
Harnessing mind-states to control thought
To mine every mind into the ritual of rot
Historical fiction, on a civilizing mission
Craft religion is the sign of your Kross
Bound up and tied together now, preying
With god
Constituents in business for progress

June Barefield

Signal distress to redress the oppressed
Bound up and tied together now
Preying with god
A process
To achieve the needs of the Beast
The beast knows the reality
Needs us all to believe
The inversion
Free our collective mind
Embrace the hive
Conversely, actual reality, a consternation design
Because free is not what it means
A slavery disease
Freedom

New faces, old lies, the Bad Magic demise

Drinking up the waters from the wells you provide
To remain parched, tasting every promise made
Still starving for truth
Confused
Gazing out into your splendor
Forgetting always to remember
But maintain somehow
For "better" days
Trying all of your love ways, feeling nothing but emptiness
Still feeling this hallowed-out place
This heaviness
Where we worked your jobs, just to endure
Still, we're poor
We die in your wars
Still, more wars
We've obeyed your law, wanting only to get along
Still, we desire peace
And dignity
We listened while you spoke about peace
Without dignity
For control
Without clarity
And still, there's but talk without change or dignity
Purely want

Stay Human

Wanting, alone
And lonely
Whispering about progress
Rule makers fix the game, the process
Mind takers shatter minds, remade in the mold, easiest to control
Making demands to supplement the soul of man
To the insane
Weeping in nightmares
Trained by the wolves to abide the howling hounds
Or be fugitives
In the land of dropping dimes
For thoughts chained to the mines where dreamers dream
Compliant to the minds where plots are schemed
Bad Magic
Authority simply means what it means
The industrial forked tongue, mainstream, red carpet rug
Pulled out from under reality
Where the old train the young
Slavery incorporated
Stolen inheritance, Progress for profit, Competition contrived

New faces, old lies
The Bad Magic demise

"The oppressed suffer from the duality which has established itself in their innermost being. They discover that without freedom, they cannot exist authentically. Yet, although they desire authentic existence, they fear it. They are at one and the same time themselves and the oppressor whose consciousness they have internalized. [. . .]"

Paulo Freire (1921-1997)

Brazilian educator and philosopher

Stay Human

The City

She's loveliest about dusk
Her's, a life lived in defiance of nature,
Nurtured by way of ambition, deception, and annihilation
Mass consumption is her function,
Sanctioned by the insane
Complete with her soundproof walls and 64" flat television screens,
Her satellite towers and lending machines,
Her surveillance cameras and 7-11 dreams
The city.

She knows not charity
In the early evening, when death rattles the spine
When the crowds move elbow to asshole, compacted together, but apart,
Driven by loneliness
Where the delusion is so strong that the grub worm takes on wings "believing" he can fly
While the bright red gory empire of men has no meaning, aside from monetary gain
Or what next one may buy
Moments disappear,
Populace unaware
The city.

Crowds of human beings, teamed together on the pavement like we'll dressed mimes
The minds of men race and dance, identifying themselves with her gorgeous annihilation
And created whim
Right around nightfall, the Crows begin to boast
The Raven cackles with a gigantic grin
Tiny robins swoop down to find cover, singing out as the Sun dips under
Returning her (the city) back to the streets,
And only the streets truly know
The city.

The death racket begins to end with spontaneous human combustion
A sort of dream flickering out and dying in her ghastly brilliance
A continuous performance daily, from b4 dawn til dusk and beyond, with no intermission
The city in all of her loveliness pants with that 5 o'clock sweat
From the tops of skyscrapers in a corrugated sky, choking out the light
Her ugly, so lovely right around dusk

June Barefield

Plan your escape you must from
The city.

It's called a "Smart City" because you would not want to live there
If they called it a "Concentration Camp."

Anything

Mediocrity rules, only the timing shifts
Mostly, people deal from the same ole' worn down deck of tricks, piecing together similar agendas of unhappiness
From the bottom of the stack, hiding the miraculous
As the clouds roam and banter across darkened skies, in the daylight of a popular lie
Our shadows chase the sun
Them say, "anything is possible"
I just cock my gun.

Mostly life is a put on, a flim-flam job, a con
A man-made dream where barely deviating schemes compete
Under the alabaster synthetic of the cities' gleam, and phony luster
Made picture-perfect, pretending that every leaf that falls is not genuinely flawed Beautiful, like God
So, the sun rises to shine, awakening the day on twelve-hour shifts with no overtime pay,
Come what may
But my anger and my resentment never melt away, not fully
A pitiful shame am I
Seems again, I am down to my very last gamble
So, all the bets are placed in an insane scramble of hope and reverence
And a dreamy-eyed ignorance
I've got no cab-fare left, or meal money to gather up together tomorrow's strength
No remaining pit stops
This is where the game stops
I've spent a lifetime allowing mediocrity to hide the miraculous
Under city lights
On this racetrack made out to be life
Full of maniacs, monsters, and spite
Them always say that "anything is possible"
But me?
I just cock my gun.

Lantern

I was sad
With good reason
Sad I was,
Growing pangs for painful days
Because sometimes what you think it is, it really ain't
Just the same, I was sad,
Hiding my anguish,
Unaware that love is language
Completely oblivious
& selfish
I'd been betrayed
I was anxious and afraid
I felt ashamed
So naturally, I'd turn my confusion into anger
Somehow, comfortable in anger
I learned anger from angry people angrily,,
Like being handed an anchor, when *I needed a lantern*
To maybe see me through this sadness
Grow past this madness
To feel the pain of it completely
All of it
Learn the lesson of it
And leave it behind
To grow
But instead,
I pointed every finger
Away from myself
I think they call it the "blame game," that's what I played
But most days, it was easy enough to just pretend I was ok
Justifiably insane
I felt it necessary to just fake
Whiskey bottle in toe
A bitter counselor for a pitiful soul
Suffering all alone, even in crowded rooms, growing cold
And fear is so flagrant once it grabs a hold.
This I now know
I'm told that betrayal is the first truth on the road of the capable
Even so, I chose this road

Stay Human

Anchor in toe
Dragged it along with the rest of my stuff, holding onto anger
An anchor
My lifeboat sinking slow
And all I was . . .
I was just sad.

June Barefield

Down Here

There is love and there is joy and there is peace and there is
"Down here"
Down here, peace is war
Down here, HOPE is eternal
It is the Bible that tells us so
Everyone always keeping tabs, calculating the score
Like "god"
Down here, with the love and the joy, only survival survives
No less
No more
No lies
Down here
Fearful chikens run from coop to coop knowing the rooster's plight
Down here
Perhaps they don't know
Perhaps them just naively unaware
Or just unprepared
Because death won't die
Down here
I've attempted to murder the conniver myself a thousand times
Death won't die
Down here
What else is there to do
But murder another murderer that looks just like you?
Everyone's got a gun
But the pawn with the gun is so quickly outgunned
Undone
Like love
I don't see none
Not down here
I've intently watched pure innocence leave my own child's eyes
Down here, he has begun to realize
Death is life
Down here, he must survive
With the love and the joy and the peace
Down here, with life
I love you, Kaleb, survive.

A Dream

It wasn't a dream

It was a possibility

To struggle

To dismantle the structures

Create our own reality

To rediscover self-reliance and determination

To change the reality

To make a difference

To believe differently in the possibility of our reality

It wasn't a dream

We were awake.

Unhappy Savage

Last night, I killed a cop
Dropped him at the corner of **29th** & Fuck the Police Lane
Brained the brainwashed, maniacal, lil piglet
Hit him in his face with them hollow point tidbits
Turned what mind he had into juicy, black partisan niblets
The BIG BAD WOLF in the blue suit now just like me & you
Unhappy
A savage.
Had him holding his little dick, hollering, try'na cover up as he squealed
I wonder if he ever wondered how it feels on the opposite end of the steel
I wonder if his mother can recover, but some hurt just never heals
I left a note on his throat as he choked back his life
It read "an eYe 4 an eYe," then I shot him in his right cheek.
It turned
The other cheek.
It turned.
Head bounced off the concrete.
In the distance, the battle cry rang out as I made my retreat . . .

"NO JUSTICE, NO PEACE!"
"NO JUSTICE, NO PEACE!"
"NO JUSTICE, NO PEACE!"

Can you feel my heartbeat?

Stay Human

A Time to Kill

Something about a city just makes you want to kill
Something about those men in masks and blue suits with shiny buttons in combat boots
Makes you want to kill

Something about my very existence makes me want to kill
My varied existence, the very reason that they kill

Something about a skin too dark, a tongue too tangled, features too foreign
Something about public lavatories and toll booths, fire engines and police sirens
Always racing down the avenues makes you want to kill

Something about boredom and fear and strife that's painted on all the faces
Chained to buses and jobs, wages and laws, like slaves in cages
Makes you want to kill

Something about a pie-faced Negro holding up a protest sign, scribblings with the women
His scenario made only a scenery for his surroundings, barely conscious of his condition
Flabby and weak, underneath the flag of imperialist elites, shivering like prostitutes
In the streets, hollering out, "I CAN'T BREATHE, I CAN'T BREATHE!"
Makes you want to kill

Something about the drum that beats inside the vacant loft of too many souls
Including my own
Something about the sun that melts anger and harassment into murder
Something about those who integrate to separate that seems desperate and temperate
Something about those who emigrate to be overseen by dark angels, spinning like tops
Controlled by evil princes makes you want to kill

Something about my very existence, insisting that I kill
My *varied* **existence**
The very reason that they kill

"Peace be still."
My meditation **whispers** to me in a dream i have, but I am completely awake.
Now is not the time.
Ever aware that there is a time . . .
A time **2** kill.

June Barefield

Turn It Off!

Promising and then menacing
Dangerous and all-encompassing
I am becoming something I cannot recognize; so, I'm running
From myself into a world of blasphemy, full of imagery
A world prepared for me by society, a civilized mockery, mocking me
The world taunts me because I am unaware of the world in me
Undaunted and desperate, I return to the old familiarity of my original haunts
Troubled inside my own thoughts
I see things
Sense things
I get drunk to try and turn it off
Sleep it off
Free for a time, but I cannot shake it off
I try, but I do not know how
I cannot shake it off!
So, I get up and I continue my climb up, out, and away from the suffocation of me
Running from my thoughts
Just another hesitant waiter, wondering thru this labyrinth of inconsequential
Skin-deep, make-believe
I can see only dimly something
I know something enchanting awaits me
I long to go to the other side
I need to know
I can see twilight in the moonlight, outside the penitence of my cell
But only partially
Compelled am i to rail against this machine!
But I do not know how; so, I take it all out on niggas from the other side of town
In and out of this nightmarish dream, but I'm awake
Every conclusion foregone, and my fate is just a fairytale
What I think as truth, I hide away
I know it's all fake.
Truth is:
Destinies are written
On the backs of smitten victims, bludgeoned by life into belligerence
Promising, but then menacing, and irreverent
Another dispossessed drone am i, fed the bone them term temperance
Tampered with to place trust in this fucking sham

Stay Human

Shameful as it is
The world is mostly just show-biz, but dangerous and all-encompassing like slave ships
Thinking again that all is not lost, but honestly . . .

I just wish I could turn it off.

The Media

What is the relationship of the media to power?

"They" own the information and control it all they want," right?

What is the news but a social construct used to control you, me, him and her, and us? Controlled by so few, so easily. Define the word "news." That too has been manipulated, the very definition itself, that is. Look it up! News!!

Past, present, and future media . . .

What is the relationship of technology to society?

The great and all-powerful agency of mass communication used to facilitate thought and discussion. Thought . . . facilitated through suggestion, opening and closing pathways to the very reasoning of the human beings consuming it. In many instances, technology, as it pertains to the media, can be used to stifle or advance the progress of what they call "civilization."

One must **define** civilization.

"They" often vulgarize and debase humanity by endangering the peace in the world, the media. "They" can play up or down the news and its significance, the media. "They" can even ignore news that is happening in our world so that, ultimately, the people remain ignorant of it. The news can be used by those who control it to foster and feed emotions one way or the other; even to make up whole fictions through the creation of often-repeated empty slogans. A change that's **never** to be believed in, the media.

Who are the persons in control of the corporations that own and direct this Behemoth, the media?

The scope and power of media increases everyday as new technology becomes available. Today, the "media" can spread lies further and faster than them people referred to as the forefathers ever dreamed of when enshrining The Freedom of the Press in the First Amendment to that Constitution people eulogize all the time. A great, great idea . . . the Constitution; if, in fact, you are of European descent and a man. The Constitution, as far as I can tell, ain't never been anything but a rich man's control measure. Do you see?

The mass media today is the major function used to inculcate people with the beliefs and values, and the codes of behavior that will integrate the individual into the institutional structures of a larger society. To fulfill this role where the concentration of wealth has created major class interest conflicts, requires the **systematic propagandizing** of the people. The news media in our minds, "we believe," is a tool that we as human beings use for the betterment of this life game, for information and knowledge. Ultimately, though, the news media is using us. The toilet is getting so much harder to flush too, but flush we must! The media. Turn that bullshit off!

Her

Sister
My protection
A reflection
Of me
Unprotected
Ever aware that I was not aware
Sister
Unafraid and prepared
For whatever
Always
Respected
Sister
Her
Always watching the cats
Surveying the rats
Beating back the dogs
And she held my hand
My connection
To the aether
The elements
Her
Too true to protect her own heart
Sister
Protected mine
My connection
Forever
Her
Forever, Eva Maria
Thank you, sister, I love you.

June Barefield

Not Forever

Our descent into matter is mostly just claptrap and blather
Where roads cross and minds are lost
In a series of imaginary negatives,
Ideology is what poisons the human being
Ideology is the creation of the ever-changing, never-changing ledger
Center-facing, but never better
A de facto involution solution
And clever
Never considering The Halls of Amenti
A 5th element-type infusion
Ignorance, the blissful dis-ease, grown into disillusion
Following monkeys
Like the idiots useful enough to murder children for the elite
Dogs follow
Trained to attack!
The soldier salutes!
The people believe
A series of negatives in
Disharmony
Under the spell of a compliant delusion
Worldwide
Following orders, murderous orders
This, our descent into matter
Where paths are crossed
And minds are lost
But not forever
No.

Stay Human

i see

To me, "God" is like a Great White Shark. White because he's "god"; a shark because i can see all of his parasites attached. This Great White, he's indifferent, like God, stroking aimlessly towards perdition. i can see him, although my vantage point is not tremendous. Normally, that advantage goes to those whose observations naturally are just keener due to the elevations at which they observe. The advantage is never provided to the underserved. Them, like "god", would refer to me as *the undeserved.* But fuck god, i observe. i see a Great White Shark, "god" of this earth, parasites attached. i see, and i possess the will to see more, see better, and i know that in the knowing i must do better. i see through the trap set for me and mine; so, i know that time in this place has no meaning.

Conversely, i have only time; so, i study you individually, and i study you in the herd, the swarm, in hordes and droves. i study the multitudes as they multiply, consecrated in the diatribe, and afraid, trapped in sameness. i see clearly the rigid outlines of your buildings which will be crumbled tomorrow, and seared through to only ash in fire and smoke. i study your "peace" programs which were started in a hail of gunfire as the ends that justify your all mighty means, and ameri**k**an dreams, all of which are but nightmares for me. i wonder about all of the people out on Main Street. That 19 year-old man-child in the Infantry, *naive, and eager to please,* like me. The insufferable ones worldwide who participate and accept this fraud. i can see it all, and i am past hope.

Once upon a time, a time that seems so far away from me now, i was hopeful. But what is simply is, and that is okay, because i can see what it really is, and it's never what you say. So, i watch, i see you so clearly these days. i know that the atom bomb, like God, is not a respecter of persons. Ever the contrarian, i do not respect you! Like "God", i see that Uncle Sam is just a criminal. **The Great White Shark**, god of this earth. i see, and i wonder why the righteous squirm so vigorously, why the high price for security, why the wars, and all the rumors of wars, and more wars? Mother ameri**K**a, i see the bitch spreading disaster for **k**apital.

i see.

Believing somehow that a person can change **T**he **S**ystem is mere fantasy. Change must come from within. '**Fuck the system**' seems a reasonable enough first thought, and now, this *change* may begin . . . u see?

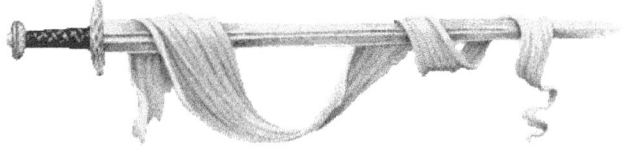

"If you tremble with indignation at every injustice, then you are a comrade of mine."

Che Guevara (1928-1967)

Argentinian revolutionary, physician, author, diplomat, and military theorist

Stay Human

Beethoven

I think Beethoven is God
Or the devil
Or maybe God is the devil
Beethoven?
Maybe Beethoven's just heaven
The third level
Heaven
Either way, I don't care
Not for God or her devil
I don't care
We need more Beethoven down here
"YOU HEAR!"

June Barefield

Earth, Moon & Pyramid

Straight lines for concentric circles
Circling the square and squaring the circle
A vibration of harmony into creation
Time squared
    a revelation
Traced into diagonals for diamonds, searching out the Nines for alignment
    in contemplation
A seekers equation
For elevation of mind
Connecting bridges into life for summation
And there are levels like ladders ascending into consciousness
From 23 to 46
From zygote to blastocyst
Earth, moon and pyramid
    a gift
Straight lines for concentric circles
Circling the square and squaring the circle

Season

Wish I knew who you were.

I wish I knew who I was back when we were.

We are no more.

In a season for scattering stones,

I scattered them all.

It was me, dearest Laniya.

Forgive me.

June Barefield

I Know

The reason the world is fucked up
It's because money buys everybody
Everywhere
All the time
It's the reason politicians have at least 8 faces
Why coonery is the cacophony the black man chases
Didn't u know?
It's the very reason your waitress wears lipstick
Why poetry in my eyes is twisted, and so-called poets hang out in groups
With their groups for protection
Lifted & listless
Why misfits remain shiftless, and musicians disappear with a mutha fuckin' quickness
Everything
Everywhere
All the time
It's just business
So, just keep all that "friend" shit
I mean . . .
If there were no money, we would all be rich, huh?
Give me the unsung every time
Fuck the Gung ho
Give me that tattooed, confused, wretchedly antagonistic, wonderfully illuminated
Truth stream.

Follow me now . . .
Because I've spent the entire night constructing my dream, but when morning
Finally arrived
The Light, again, it blinded me
There are these long streams of light, organs of insight, braided tightly into my future
Even in complete darkness
Always, there is Light
Sutured and sewed up for me is a destiny for the FREE!
I know
All the imperfect pictures painted recklessly in the delusions of my past
Finally, I've turned my back on its pull
Shit, I know only the Jester and the fool will tell the KiNg the truth
They understand the reason that the entire world is fucked up!
Everybody

Stay Human

Everywhere
All the time
So, I just spit breath mists of introspection in order to create a personal cave for my soul
Dredging up the old sadness, just to add them to the new
In the shadows of the masked and the damned
In the city, jam-packed, sitting next 2 the man, who's sitting next to the man,
Sitting next to the man
A competition of comparisons
Every persona made in ameriKa
Bossed up, tryna be "the man"
Nigga, fuck the man!
I'm try'na join the Taliban!!
I write poetry, play chess, and pound my boney lil chest, never hiding the miraculous
Ever.
Foolish, foolish, foolish, me!
I know the reason the world is fucked up!

June Barefield

Men Must Act

My words, I am able to arrange
Seasons change strangely these days, but the world keeps spinning
Beginning again at the ending
The only real decision to be made is about the living, and the suffrage
A search to find meaning
A very strange sort of division
Duality twisted
Sanity pending
But life is also a rhythm
A conscious choice about care and giving, and loving with intention
Forever driven by the fact that there is no obstacle anywhere insurmountable
Men must act!
Admittedly, at times, I question this fact
Moved too often by my own lack of insight
Curiosity somehow feeding indecision
Coupled with an ill will, confiding in derision
An opposite polarity condition
Driven by something that should not feel so strange
"Hope"
But come what may, there are words
So very strange are words and life and tears and fears to strive
For love
So, I've learned the "safe" way
I just crush my smiles inside
I stifle my screams so that I won't cry
Stoically, I dream my dreams though
Delightfully inviting, always, this dream I dream
A pleasant, quiet dream
A dream of life and wonder and a peace that is everlasting
An idea complete with laughter
Mostly, these ideas of mine gesticulate, remaining mostly unborn
Torn, I pray for my own unfaithfulness in scorn
The flimflam in the scam that is religion
The wretchedness
The skin games, sworn to make the lie credible
The images
Nothing anywhere's ever what it appears to be, especially me
Unaware, I walk thru another door

Stay Human

Completely unaware
In the hands of some unseen power
Words I devour, arrange
and continue to explore
Life's still just a crapshoot
So, I shake 'em up and I roll 'em out on the floor
And 7even's still the truth, or so I'm told
Too many times in this life, all that's come up is 6ixes
For me, all the time, everywhere, just 6ixes
Always, am I deciding the disconcerting
Decisions, decisions, and more decisions; along with, of course, more 6ixes
For me and mine, 'The Deuce' has always been high; so, we let the mutha' fuckas ride, Right?
Convinced inside that there's nothing anywhere living or dead that will change
The hearts of men
I roll 'em again!
After all . . .
There is NO obstacle anywhere at all that is insurmountable
Always there is what them call possibility and the accompanying
Coexisting probabilities
A corresponding vibration to protect us from what we "think" is calamity
Intuitively, I see the variables of conspicuous inconsistency hiding in plain sight
Always so agile and polite
But something in their eyes
In the spirit
The energy
It lies
No worries tho', I've got this rift in my mind
This tiny opening surrounded by light
A peculiar sort of compatibility
A wonderfully uninhibited place where sparks rip the sky in my mind's eYe
Moving gracefully through poisoned waters, forgetting nothing
Forgiving all
Call it "The magic of life"
Connectivity
Electricity
Vibration
Positive polarity for energies
Again, pendulums swing,
Forcing me into another decision
So, again, I begin, penciling in words

June Barefield

My words, I am able to arrange
Every inclination worth stating, a return to words
Always for me, it is words
I write
Words, I arrange
Driven by hope
Praying for a change that first must begin in me
Within me
This, the orientational intent, to begin each day
Wondering always about the hearts of men
Men like me
The seasons are changing so strangely these days
But again, in the end

MEN MUST ACT!

New Illusion

Subjugated to my suffering, surrendering systematically
Dissipated and demoralized inside this vegetative state where another well-disguised
Ill-advised, plate of disingenuous hate has been processed
And in the process of my processed mind-state, I stay processing the process, wondering
How long the process takes?
Outside forces got me living in the **RED**
Walking amongst the blind, in the midst of the living dead
Fed a convoluted truth since my disgruntled youth
And there is no counterbalance on these here-scales
Everything's for sale everywhere
So, I've bought up enough truth to make believe I can undo what I've done, and maybe
See a new sun
Sifted in amongst the shiftless
Part of the schematic and systematically inconsistent
I missed another shift amongst the gifted
A peculiar sort of misfit
Feeling ANIMALISTIC and sadistic
Twisted and unlisted
Always this return to the listless
My reality, a prison that I myself am choosing
I've gotta break it down now
Create a new illusion.

Kingly Conception

Who invented this concept,
Time?
& Seconds inside minutes
& Hours inside days
DATES?
& Days inside months
YEARS?
Our fears
All of them encapsulated and contained W/I the boundaries of these circles
Once a venerated benevolent people
UNEQUALED
4500 years B4 any copycat messianic messages reinvented the reGaL
Remember?
The white boy council at Nicea
Constantine and him peoples.

Originally, conception was Kingly
Then come immaculate deception . . . bring in the sequel
Eradicate an entire people's recollection
Nation by nation
Generations effaced
Made to be Xhristian
Given new names, then erased
A debasement, this jesus replacement.

The Empress Queen Isis birthed a Royal, reGaL, KINGLY SuN
Thus, the pride of "civilized" life had long since begun
Sung heavenly tunes in tones of gold and silver and RED and violets of blue
All from the hue of you
BLACK.

A mastered ASTROLOGICAL place
In time and space, seconds, minutes, hours
& Days
But dates?
Now them call u negro!
Them murder you
Maim you

Stay Human

Rape your sister
Remove your father
And now negro, you cannot stand to look at your own face
Think it safe to imitate this evil
Call it self-hate
But maybe it is Maybeline?
Perhaps the integrated AMERIKAN slave wish to now don his Emperor's cape?
Comfortable and warm
Unaware of the SUN
Blind to the incoming storm
Conformity, complex completion for societal norms
The Black skin white mask put on
Too many iLL-conceived misdeeds being spun
From Ethiopia's oldest daughter Egypt
Dealt an artless hand of dupery
Influences now external . . . myth made memory for the amalgamation of "WE"
Because there is no "US"
Just time
& Days inside years
Frightened by truth
Circled by fear
The mulatto problem itself, a boiling vat of pork fat and unrighteous acts
More malicious scraps of fictitious frenzy way B4 the Dawn arrives
And in the eyes of God?
A thousand years as one day
And in 6 days
This conception, time
In God's time
Sublime
Seconds inside minutes
& Dates
Hours inside days
Generations effaced
Nation by nation
What we've accepted as history is minus "The People of the Sun"
The Semitic storms of Axum
The mighty Empress, **Queen Candace**
This wicked fantasy invention
An investment, like stock in prisons
But originally
Conception was Kingly

June Barefield

And in time . . .

Cast into a realm, dreadfully transformational
The hubbub of the legal disputation
Merely a transaction for the desperate peasant lacking direction
Tryna balance what u do with who you are
Infected
From possibility to actuality
Impractically influenced by the idea of US
Within, where the real enemies' energy enters
Wasting time
Seconds inside minutes
Hours inside days
Dates erased
Days inside months replaced
Generation after generation debased
Once a venerated benevolent people
Follow me now . . .

Originally, conception was Kingly
. . . And in time

Stay Human

Little Man

Born into a facade, lacking any luxury at all
Tiny bits and pieces of Lil man can be found
From the ground up
Reflecting in the faces of the sick, too poor 4 hospital visits
Or in the detainees, and prisoners
Prisoners of a war that *Jim Crow* only ignores
Where human beings of Lil man's stature are policed
From station to station, basement to basement
Warehoused in this new aged enslavement
This system
And if one listens . . .
You'll hear, then find pieces; fractured broken bits and pieces
Inside the vernacular of the UN-spectacular
These over-anxious passengers, just passing by through life
Lives whose very architecture is . . .
LITTLE man.

From his infancy into toddler-ship
Ill-equipped & unfit, but still, a beautiful, brave, husky, rugged, handsome little hopper
Face square, expression tense; eyes, a wildfire, unsmiling and beguiling
His spirit already filled up with hurt
Anger blazing within this hurt, this pain . . . his Rage
Staging a defense for all
A defense for the ages
LITTLE man.

Carefully, he absorbs all of his lessons in the street
He's not learning arithmetic, to write or to read
At an early age, a hustler is he; if only to eat
Just learning the game and then loving the game, but ultimately, he too, he'll be played
By the game
A game where black lives, always less valuable than white property
So, properly . . .
The monies meant for Lil man's publiK education, spent to build prisons
And this is where he expects to go
He's never been given a real chance to grow
2B

June Barefield

In balance and peace
LITTLE man.

Inside these lines, confessed
We all know little man, but perhaps we cannot see
Little man is a picture painted for us all so imperfectly
Admittedly, his canvas, a bit torn, ripped, and jagged around the edges
Our creation is he
A creation of factual sations and unloving relations
His picture survival, in an environment unrivaled, if not for the police
Instinctively impulsive
Instructively destructive, and it's his aggression mostly that speaks
He's got to be a man too soon, but a man, indeed
Our little transplanted seed of infamy; inside this mushrooming oasis of infidelity
This treachery, his unreliable reality, where there is no elixir
No purgatory
No escape from the streets.
LITTLE man.

For Robert & Karlos
Rest in Peace

4NOW

UNDERLING IMP: "Would you like to kill him or damage him,
Control him a bit or just manage him?"

DEMON: "Ultimately, death, of course, is the answer, but for now . . .
I prefer him locked up
Ñ a jail
Inside of a cell
Behind bars is where his futile little game stops, you understand?
Ñ a jail
Inside a cell
Locked away
Behind bars."

DEMON: "I want him up when I tell him
He can eat what we feed him
He'll move when he's instructed to, and stop when I tell him to
Walk him to the field, a mill, or factory, and then work him until he understands
His Master's plan
If he chooses 2B defiant, smack his face
Beat him whenever it pleases you to do so
Anything and everything that may possibly represent an independence of
Spirit & mind, must be broken
I want you to break him!"

DEMON: "I want him locked, strapped, stopped, but alive, for now
I want his entire bloodline subservient
I want the mother of his children alone in the ghettos of Amerika, in project pens without
Him, so that she obediently accepts the meager scraps we provide her, and learns to hate
Him
Usher his ass into a permanent 2nd class status
Dismantle him completely from our little 'civilized' apparatus
Develop for him, if you will, a sort of parallel universe, with absolutely no real, tangible
Exit ramps

Here is where he and all of his croniesare—how do they say . . . Homies
ALL THE BLACK BASTARDS embrace my curse, do my work, and die a black nigger!"

June Barefield

UNDERLING IMP **(a black man)**: "Yes, boss."

DEMON: "Of course, I want to kill him
I want the entire black nigger population; preferably the black male nigger, dead
But first . . .
We will destroy him
I want him locked away from everything he loves
Ñ a jail
Inside of a cell
Behind bars.
4NOW."

Stay Human

Eugenics. The End Game: Population Control

"The best men must cohabit with the best women in as many cases as possible, and the worst with the worst in the fewest, and that the offspring of the one must be reared and that of the other not, if the flock is to be as perfect as possible." Plato (*Republic*, Book 5).

"It does not, however, seem impossible that by an intention to breed, a certain degree of improvement, similar to that among animals, might take place among men." Thomas Malthus, 1798.

"Eugenics is the study of the agencies under social control that may improve or impair the racial qualities of future generations either physically or mentally." Francis Galton, 1883.

"I wish very much that the wrong people could be prevented from breeding; and when the evil nature of these people is sufficiently flagrant, this should be done." Theodore Roosevelt ("Twisted Eugenics," in *The Works of Theodore Roosevelt*, op. cit., National Edition, XII, p. 201).

"Birth control must lead ultimately to a cleaner race." Margaret Sanger, 1922.

"We should hire three or four colored ministers, preferably with social-service backgrounds, and with engaging personalities. The most successful educational approach to the Negro is through a religious appeal. We don't want the word to go out that we want to exterminate the Negro population." Margaret Sanger, 1939.

"There are three ways of securing a society that shall be stable as regards population. The first is that of birth control, the second that of infanticide or really destructive wars, and the third that of general misery except for a powerful minority." Bertrand Russell, 1953.

"It will be important for UNESCO to see that the eugenics problem is examined with the greatest care, and that the public is informed of the issues at stake so that much of what now is unthinkable may at least become thinkable." Julian Huxley, 1946.

"In order to stabilize the world population, we must eliminate 350,000 people per day. It is a horrible thing to say, but it is just as bad not to say it." Jacques Cousteau, 1991.

This is a plan that is being formulated as you read the cited words above. For centuries, the controlling oligarchy and those placed in the position to influence the masses have been incrementally culling the world's population. Recently, what we called "The Georgia Guidestones" was vandalized and subsequently torn down. 500,000,000 is the number of human beings that your controllers require to, as they said, "keep the planet in perpetual balance with nature."

June Barefield

Your heroes are not necessarily who you thought they were, huh?

. . . But Apart

Boulevards unravel for the nameless ones
And shell games are played
Like a broken Englishman's servants cascade, where Negros promenade
And dark men darken the darkened
Blinded by the great white domes of ill enlightenment
Frightened, but fighting to fit in
So the streets they spill into
A spell casted by *Jim Crow* innuendo for the see-through
And maybe, you do love life alive, out of spite
Out of sight, sound, in silence
Wound up, severed in violent cycles
Bound together in unholy alliances
DEFIANCE DEFINED!
By men with broken English, riding narrow walkways like subway trains
Again, and then, over again
This insanity, expanding just like the shell games played as nameless faced men
Begin again spilling out onto the streets on a killing spree
Milling about now in stables for the fabled, incorrigible, unlearned label
For the felon
Folded favorably in sections
Like an unpretty untruth in flights, connecting
Kites inside the mired mirror of rejection
Reflecting the midnight of unraveled boulevards
A hopelessness
An incompetent ignorance
Cognitively dissonant
. . . but **ACTIVE**
In pen blocks
On pen yards
Together, but apart
Commuters in dark bland coats
Cutthroat
And now . . .
Blinded by the Great White Domes of Travertine
Traversing yellow lines, but only on the right side
Riding these narrow pathways like metro trains
Bunched together, but apart

June Barefield

Waiting to spill out again onto the streets
Another killing spree
FREE!
Blinded by The Great White, cutthroat notion of Travertine
Traversing endlessly
In tragedy.

Stay Human

Ruin

Beyond the point

Beyond which anybody can go

Where two crevices crisscross on cracked pavement under an April moss

Lost.

Underneath labyrinths of sky-scraped, ticker-taped gloss

Tossed by winded images of want and ruin

Waiting and watching from dark doorways and empty window panes

Pained by the same relentless, cold, indifferent kiss from God

In vain.

Up and down hard streets, crawling with spite and shame

Smitten, while fools rush into and out of unexplored corridors, ignored

Beyond the point

Beyond which anybody can go.

Define Freedom

Is it a destination, an anecdotal potion, sold by the portion validating this notion? Freedom. Generally speaking . . . what sort of clever tricks must one perform, curtsying in a suit and tie for this curated con job, co-signed to be consigned to oblivion, integrated with demons, assuming your destination B Freedom? Essay, if you dare, an explanation. DEFINE FREEDOM.

Stay Human

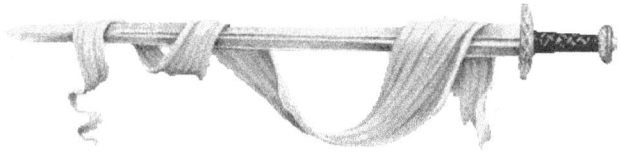

"Voting, the be all and end all of modern democratic politicians, has become a farce, if indeed it was ever anything else. By voting, the people decide only which of the oligarchs preselected for them as viable candidates will wield the whip used to flog them and will command the legion of willing accomplices and anointed lickspittles who perpetrate the countless violations of the people's natural rights. Meanwhile, the masters soothe the masses by assuring them night and day that they — the plundered and bullied multitudes who compose the electorate — are themselves the government."

Robert Higgs (b. 1944)
American economic historian and economist

My Urban Analysis
An Observation

A sort of dislocated destitute destiny
Never defined
Blind to this fate
I've magnified the institutional lie, clutching it closely, "believing" it mine
Look into my eyes
Black SPARK white FIRE
An inherited generational paralysis
Defiance alive
Spirit at war
Soul slowly dying
Meantime . . .
The civilized, they bumble together in a heap of catatonic hysteria
Sadly hysterical
I observe
Every complexion colored with the language of politi**K**
A systematized indoctrination covet
Lightly tickled, entertaining one's analytical pleasure buttons
Society is a spectacle
"Folk tales of the Amur"
A bunch of nickel slick exhibition
Some call it 'culture'
Others 'tradition'
But what it is:
Sedition from the NATURAL
Each contradiction contrasting the so-called "Christian"
Factual constriction of spirit
Call it "Religion"
Give ye unto Caesar, Negro!
STATISM, the revision
Sedation for a nation of responsible consumers
Watching and following
Swallowing up all of the poison, one cup at a time
And there are levels like ladders descending into oblation
Enter ye into the asylum now!
Assimilation Nation
Indoctrination station

Stay Human

Create for one's self a brand new illusion
I observe
Inside myself:
Introspective reflections in only shattered mirror shards where an empty cadaver
With angry eyes stares back, confused
So, in these shallow waters, we wade
Where the blackest face possesses the whitest mind, shedding the skin of time in waves
Trained up in the way, afraid
The Mass Mind in total compliance
eYe observe
Them obey
And I'm thinking that I am "they". . .

June Barefield

Culture & Law

There will always be a small minority who refuse to obey the tenets of cultural law. Because of this, authorities employ a constant stream of violence known as "law enforcement" or "police." These are not police in defense of liberty, but police in defense of authority. Cultures always teach that liberty and authority are one and the same, but the purpose of the police is to wield the weapons of violence in the preservation of authority, not to defend liberty.

When cultures begin to break down, it is because people are learning about their value. Such cultures and the authorities they protect are doomed. Never once in history has a culture in decline been redeemed. Not once! So, when the so-called authorities see that their culture is being dismantled, and that control over the masses begins to suffer, and the obedience of the people is no longer theirs to enjoy, they return to violence. These returns to violence are historically extremely brutal. I believe that the violent enforcement of law is a sign of coming liberty.

The sole objective of law is obedience, and the destruction of freedom is found in the blindness of this obedience. **The authority principle** shows that even when a person would normally "believe" an action to be morally wrong, if ordered by an authority, they will still perform it. Ask any veteran of foreign conflict, or a police dummy, used in such a flagrant manner throughout history to serve and protect the property of their controllers. I call these "good people," useful idiots, or more poignantly, attack dogs for the rich.

The law only holds any real value for those who've created it, and only because your "culture" demands that you obey it. And so, if The People be comfortable enough, then **culture** is not only obeyed, but celebrated.

Culture is part of the mechanism that creates a mindframe, easily manipulated for control and propagandizing. The purest invitation to tyranny is your commitment to obey the law, regardless of what it says, and fuck culture! Against you, the law becomes the perfect weapon. Whoever controls the law, controls you, and at a level in society so easily controlled. Our worth is measured by the extent of our obedience to The State. **Conformity to law** is culture. So much so that it's treated as a virtue.

For instance, the citizen in our fair ameriKa is proud of being extorted, and thinks it is right-minded and upright, morally correct even, to pay his or her taxes. So much so that paying these state-sponsored extortion fees is a point of contention, wrongfully separating human beings against themselves for the betterment of no one except those in control. Last time I checked, General Electric pays zero in taxes! An absolute unadulterated tyranny.

Society, through culture, created by law, mostly, is a mere spectacle. A joint-stock company, if you will, wherein each shareholder knows in order that his monies to remain secure and ever-expanding, the obedient commoner must, time and again, surrender his liberty, secure in the control and virtuous conformity he competes for. Self-reliance is ever the aversion to law, to culture.

Stay Human

No Us

Inculcated the entirety of the world into the basement of reasoning
The perpetually me, only me, thinking the thoughts fabricated for me, and i am you
So, together we play the fool
Right from the beginning
With the 12 years of school and the lofty dreamscape of college
We, together, have all been duped into this religion of selfishness lacking
Any true knowledge
A macrocosmic gift, call it the arbitrary morality under which the peasant class must live
Braced and binded
Blinded by lofty hopes of increase
A client, all of us, in compliance, ever reliant on the constructs of a mind molded for only
Repetitive compulsions
Looked over and locked out
Repulsive, in the eyes of the real controllers
The human mind is in crisis
The fishbowl is full of the lifeless, preyed upon so cleverly, extolled and lauded
Applauded for obedience, and tethered together "heavenly"
But "Lucifer is God"
The Possessor
Enchanter
The destroyer
On a civilizing mission
Building the institutions to assimilate your children into a house on fire
To make them "us"
If you have eyes to see, you must not "believe"
If you have ears to hear, you must NOT be deceived
Civilized minions, bowing and bending the knee, essentially begging the powers that be
Allowing the tyrant to dictate what it is that this thing they told you was "freedom"
What it really means
Ask your landlord who his land-**Lord** is, then bring him to me!
Freedom must be cocked and locked, chambered and extracted
Exacted in spots like Haiti and The Congo, in Sudan, and in Nicaragua, Syria, Yemen
And of course, **Palestine**
Freedom!
A dream!
And down here on Main Street, bedlam screams out like a bitch!
The mind-state, infected

June Barefield

From possibility to actuality
Impractically influenced by the idea of 'US'
Inside, where the insidious pretends to be honorable, pivoting just left of center
Forgetting to remember
The crisis of consciousness buying up this dream
Freedom!
A shadowy illusion, prepared for us at the haberdashery factory just after dusk
But in reality, there is no 'us.'

Help Me!

Anchored firmly here on the bottom
Tethered heavenly here
On
The
BOTTOM
My dream requisite, ingestible
An acquired taste
My fate & destiny manifest too late
Here in this place
On the bottom, where i deconstruct my hate
Help me!
My fear & doubt impregnate some goofy dream deferred
A raisin in the sun ignored
Always
i keep one eYe on the bourgeois
Witness do i another deplorable compromise restored
Help me!
Here
On the
Bottom
Again, ignored
Skim do eYe lightly over the absurd
Here
On the
Bottom
Where i must choose
My choice, a trap infused
i'd be not confused
It matters not
i choose a choice already chosen 4 me
Generational, my choice

Nurtured in the fantastical!

Help me define my voice
Help me!
My inferiority is a complex

June Barefield

A germ
Worming its way thru all the limits of my ambivalence
Conditioned by blind, raging, indifference
Indifferent
Here
On the
Bottom
Reaching deeply down into the bloody red toil, enriching the soil
& For the sake of the cause, unaware, i adopt the process
Whitened by years and years of humiliation
Not my process
Inflexible 2 kneeling, i must kneel,
Kneel at the altar of my abasement
Here on the bottom, i inoculate this feeling, concealing nothing
Here on the bottom,
i dig my heels viciously into the flanks of a world not made 4 me
i watch
& i wait
My patience, a slave
Here on the bottom, tethered heavenly
Help me
Please!

TOMB

The world is in retreat; so, stay the fuck off the grass
A Chinese Nigga swallowed a wombat somewhere in Wûhan
Now the truth is in a mask
Predicament, ridiculous
Strangely cruel for the old or indigenous
The world wears "normal" at the whim of an elitist agenda
Nothing RIGHT or wrong, but thinking is what makes it so
No one believes in reality, only in thinking thoughts, manufactured by the machine
Governments lie
Banks steal
The wealthy laugh
Only mask up for television
The very surface of "being" is crumbling
My greatest delight is to walk the streets alone at night
My streets, they smell of hunger and desperation
I feel like an army of men itch to unravel their particular tale of misery
Life, slowly beginning to resemble only ruin, where willingly, we construct
Our own tombs
Stinking of dirty feet, sweat, bad breath, and lysol
The "World" is in retreat
Stay the fuck off the grass, nigga!

War

Saw you in a dream up under thundering clouds
Lightning, striking, burning everything around you down
You are crying now, but I cannot reach out
Too many thorns in the crown
This bloodied brow feels no pain, only numbness now
THE WALKING WOUNDED MUST REMAIN IN THE WAR
My dream is confusing, but I dream on,
Frozen and afraid of what's in store
Ignored by you as I scream out
I reach out to you, but you turn about
Consumed in shadow
Swallowed up in the storm
The walking wounded
Must remain
In the
WAR.

Stay Human

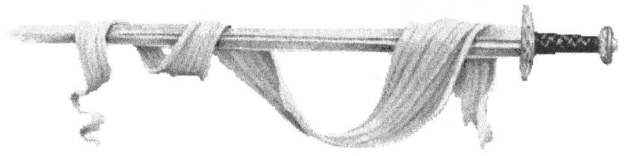

*"The Plandemic was brought in for the vaccine.
The vaccine was brought in for the vaccine passport.
The vaccine passport was brought in for the biometric ID.
The biometric ID was brought in for the Central Bank Digital Currency.
The Central Bank Digital Currency was brought in to enslave you."*

Dr. Judy Anne Mikovits (b. 1958)

American former research scientist

Look Outside

The consistent tone is just obvious
Oblivion for the commoner, merely an arrangement
An artless creation of the banal by the beastly
An unemotional functional denial in acceptance
Where apathy and reluctance recant the dysfunction,
And truth is the principal falsehood
In a fog of plausibility, where brush strokes of civility intervene cleverly
Masking integrity
The "civilized" tame, the savage masses, dumbing down the energy
Every soul modified genetically
Privately patented like the *COVID experiment*
The Master class passes out the Prozac, the Oxy, and the Fentanyl
Afghani heroine props up the failed economy
Shifting levels
A brave new World
Thought, processed for ownership
Scaffolding the spirit of men
Dreams dashed
System castes
Real connectivity, long past
Competition is king
Consumption, the task
Well-versed clowns on television wear masks
And the youth are educated to be full-fledged consumers
Customers
Each in possession of a "smart" phone, television, and Wi Fi in their very own rooms
Where comparing delusion gives compliance greater fusion
Desolation from within
From the umbilical into the upper colon, on to the hypogastric region, until
Post pineal lobes are boiled alive
Mental liquidation
A rendering tethered heavenly, where a geometrical stiffness quickens
An ideational sickness
Fuck it tho', business is booming!
But if you look outside, human kind is being slaughtered with just the right
Demented touch to give predatory power poignancy
A warm sultry haze lies over my city, like a gigantic cup of lard

Stay Human

I drop some loot in the mailbox for the young homie, still walking the yard
I pray 4 him
Life is hard
The tone, a consistent drone
& So obvious
The law-abiding citizen, oblivious
Infected with this **virus**, a **conformity** existence
Just take a look outside.

June Barefield

My Good Friend Insomnia

You fight in the light, but you must think in darkness
In silence
Quiet the chaos, and extinguish the riot
Inside, where madness shatters rationality
In stillness
To justify war and famine, and pestilence and disease
All providence, merely the pretension of thieves, but defiance resides
In stillness
Whether or not it's war
Or peace
As sure as The Dawn, defiance will rise
The eYe gathering in the storm, and stillness
One coin, two sides
A precious coin, refined by fire
For every suggestion reflected upon, but believed not
The Light for the Dark
For certain, a submersion, an extinction of self, in thought
Where the spark ignites the flame
A return to breath
The only true science to blame for the miscalculation of every rational step taken,
Forsaken with lofty fantasies of increase
"Progress" is what them call it
But again, begin
This madness shatters rationality, quietly, again
In thought for mind expansion
Where true mansions are constructed with just a handful of dust
For nothing at all
. . . *but love*
The reason for this madness . . .

Gravity

Stampeding towards the badlands in a state of panic & resentment, punishing ourselves with more empty pleasures

Ice cream dreams for fake friends in fair weather

Measured out on mystic, lacerated, lightning bolts as the stars glisten, sparkling like diamonds against a backdrop of pure darkness

But gravity explains us.

So, we stretch and bend, flex and spend our entire life longing for love, but frightened to death of it

In a lopsided, left-leaning, demeaning shuffle, through the hustle and bustle, mind muscle atrophied, feverishly "believing" in an existence where relief requires medication, and charity, paperwork

This is life . . .

So, we carry on this conversation quietly with a whisper inside of ourselves where a symphony is being played out so beautifully for the souls of men, but very few are listening.

Every heart and mind, doused in the asphyxiating, monotonous, humming drone of the **energy** and the **tone** we have chosen to live in.

Our bodies, like magnets, pull us ever closer to despair, while the slow ache of things left undone lingers in the air.

And then suddenly one day, the last true note escapes this bell, a horn of anything less than plenty, through the dark hole of forever, rising up to begin again without explanation, levitating, then escaping, finally escaping

The gravity that has defined us.

Master

Repudiating some ancient taboo thru' the eyes of the master
Trampling the ruins of our solitude
Splinter in every wound
From disaster to disaster and tomb to tomb
My so-called brother's teeth glisten at the compliments of hypocrites in gold-rimmed spectacles
Ambiguous to what them call the "black experience"
Confounded from sunrise to sunset
Blinded and dumbfounded at master's indifference
How very patient you are!
Eyes turn blue at the sound of your master's voice
How pathetic you are!
Your face, a picture painted perfectly with brush strokes of civility
Gorged now with the empty, lofty, lying words of your enemy
My shout now rings out more violently
Silently, I place the stone back into my sling
Gently easing the splinter out of my wounds
By the deceits of the master.
Now, my shout rings out much more violently.

Stay Human

"Evil then, for the moment, is the force, residing either inside or outside of human beings, that seeks to kill life or liveliness. [...]"

M. Scott Peck (1936-2005)

American psychiatrist and best-selling author

June Barefield

A Nigga

If time is relative and all of our definitions are speculative
If word connotation both confirms and denies a white man's objectives
And of course, a nigga is always the usual suspect
Tell me, who the fuck are we, really, collectively?

A nigga.
Just a bewildered, seasonless, neutral soul
Controlled
Devoid of heat or of cold
A windless, powerless collection for the splendor of another to behold
Bound by the laws and language, the traditions of another man's code
En Masse
Filled with a hopeless, demoralizing, empty terror
Imbued with the Willie Lynch gene, but NOT in error
Witlessly preoccupied, eternally subservient, weary and wary
With only these unrelenting facts of this, his nigger-ness, to recall
Blessed with, "cursed be Canaan, let God enlarge Japeth!"
Vanities' captor now, full of numbness and dread
But even our vanity we cannot own
Alone
Trained that upheaval is evil, as we raise up our freedom signs
Incorporated into this psyche, the dark half, the sequel
Second to all
Integrated into a house already ablaze, and sure to fall
Abject apologists are we, pointing the finger away from ourselves
Shuffling along with a cheap, little, grin
Motiveless, because motive requires reason
'Tis the season for Vain Glory
The story, unforgivable
Treasonous, and sorry . . .
A nigga
His glory is self-hate
And so it is
In this way
Inside of this hate, the wake of oblivion dawns for
A nigga.

All Men

We come into this world protected and pure, simple, and beautifully vacant of the contaminants that the world most assuredly will provide in time. We enter into this life miraculously human, God's gift, free of the corruption and conditioning soon to be inherited, mimicked, and brought to bear upon all we touch. Anxious to uncover the "meaning" of things, full of desire and yearning, with the putrid matter of what we're told matters, accompanied by want, and the depravity of success for secular excess.

Them say: **"Born into iniquity, raised up in sin."**

I disagree.

A necessary evil is transcribed so eloquently, written on the hearts of men. This is where we begin. From sheltered to shattered and then back again. Protected, pure, and miraculously human.

All men.

June Barefield

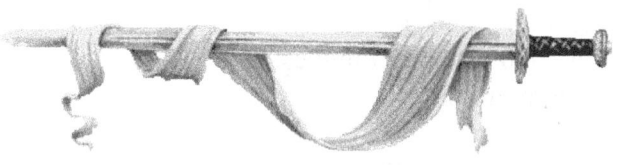

"The past is more than a memory."

John Trudell (1946-2015)

American author, poet, actor, musician, and political activist

I Think

For each flash and every flicker
A statistical vigor, status quo residual
Interactive comparisons from individual to individual
Double-decked walruses marching in a trance, calmly, to the oyster banks
A sort of bling nag delirium
Cackling together with 1000 different tongues
1000 different outfits, without wit
All the same, all undone
Singing out empty words, wired by the maniacal
Thought itself, wash-machined into the very soul of "being"
But maybe, "soul" is an incorrect descriptive
This sort of "being," merely a cruel, belligerent affliction
Inscription 500,000,000
Subtracted from 8 billion
The New Order of the World says to eliminate 7,500,000,000
Definition: **Crocodilian**
Population-control to eliminate the children
So that predatory power perverts every spirit
Civil villains "brand" everything human in unnaturalness
Invert reality
Convince them it's realness
All is contractual
Undressed with proof that's fact
But fact has no meaning
Gaslighting and double talk to control what you're thinking
To monitor what you say
Where any pursuit in critical thinking is made criminal
Follow me now . . .
CRITICAL THOUGHT IS CRIMINAL!
Dealing with cannibals, cutthroats, and demons in tailored suits, all perfumed and cute
But for the common man
For the working man
There is no absolute, ever
Fight their wars
Conduct their menial labor
Question authority, never!
Always comply
"You will own nothing, and you will be happy"

June Barefield

A Metaverse reality
Every melody impure, and the toilets getting harder to flush
Walking always against a united world, asserting only what divides us
Breathing in the fever of the day
Compliant slaves, trained to obey
This climate will never change
Statistically vigorous, obediently tuned in, checking 4 status quo residuals
Each flash and every flicker
A sort of bling nag residual
Where predatory power corrupts even the spiritual

Imagine though . . .
Once you were wild and murderous
You were free, I think.

Climate Change: The Global Warming Swindle

For 50 years or more, a devilishly clever plan has been in the making. A class war, disguised as saving the planet, is revealed as a means for the so-called elites to take over the environment, re-engineer our cities, and control our populations. The easily manipulated, forever propagated public has been induced to feel fear and confusion, shamed into believing that they're responsible for this swindle that they term "The Climate Crisis." To better control the people of the planet, bioterrorism, pandemics, and vaccinations have been implemented incrementally along the way to the ultimate goal of total dominion over all, everywhere in the world. A devilishly clever plan.

Man himself has been made out to be the planet's enemy, shamed into compliance. Humanity, coerced into believing its way of life is destructive, having been pitted against one another. Forced mass immigrations, used to dilute culture and attack traditional value systems. Climate Change. The Global Warming Swindle . . .

Seemingly truthful narratives were created, concerning pollution, environmental degradation, biodiversity loss, climate challenges, and of course, the all-powerful pandemic. All of these things working together, creating hysteria and fear, ultimately reaching the fiendish goal of a Scientific Dictatorship. At every phase along the way, the stories were twisted, the science, a lie . . . and professional, educated people went along and perpetrated this fraud. National sovereignty to be replaced by global governance. A plan incorporated over the span of at least 50yrs, each piece strategically placed in its proper place at its proper time by organizations like The Gavi Alliance, The World Economic Forum, World Health Organization, The United Nations, and others, with a common agenda termed "Sustainable Development Goals." To end poverty and hunger, for gender equality, and reduced inequalities. For clean water and affordable, clean energy, peace, justice, and strong institutions.

"Climate change," the global warming swindle, is an evil concoction developed over decades for control. In a Club of Rome publication entitled ***THE FIRST GLOBAL REVOLUTION***, written in 1991 by the wicked, pitiless, beastly fiends that control you and me, that control politicians, and own the media, the following was declared:

"The common enemy of humanity is man. In searching for a new enemy to unite us, we suggested that pollution, the threat of global warming, water shortages, famine, and the like would fit the bill. In their totality and in their interactions, these phenomena constitute a common threat that demands the solidarity of all peoples. But in designating them as the enemy, we fall into the trap about which we have already warned, namely mistaking symptoms for causes. All these dangers are caused by human intervention, and it is only through changed attitudes and behavior that they can be overcome. The real enemy then is humanity itself."

These so-called elites and organizations that conduct this long con on the world's population expect to achieve this control by taking control of 30% of the entire Earth's land and seas by the year 2030. These Luciferian globalists and their flunkies at the UN will make the claim that they have achieved worldwide consensus in implementing, into the language and ultimately into the lives of human beings living here on Earth, what they call Multilateral Solutions for a Better Tomorrow. There's a global dictatorship being foisted upon us all, and all the places where the information to gain an understanding of what's being done have been captured. To unravel ourselves from the noose, created over decades of planning and preparation, we must disobey at every level. Human beings must act, come together, and unite. There is a door to freedom that humanity must walk through to engage with the truth of the future and what these despicable people, The Elites, have planned for us. Time is getting shorter as the sand sifts through the hourglass and the door to freedom closes. All of this has been documented. It will come to pass.

My thoughts? Global warming is an international hoax, a sham for control and complete dominance over the world's entire population. All aspects of life in the 21st century are to be regulated and **taxed**. Climate Control is nothing more than a necessary step toward ultimate serfdom in a feudalistic future society. From Chile to the Antarctic, from the plains of the Savannah in Africa to the steps of Russia, what "they" want is Global Monopoly.

My thoughts? **EAT THE RICH**.

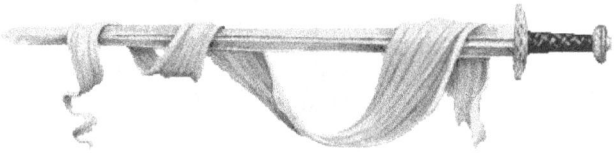

"Money, being naturally barren, to make it breed money is preposterous and a perversion from the end of its institution, which was only to serve the purpose of exchange and not of increase . . . Men called bankers we shall hate, for they enrich themselves while doing nothing." [In: *Politics*]

Aristotle (384BC-322BC)

Greek philosopher and polymath

June Barefield

Insomnia

Still thinking.
Probably should be sleeping.
Sleep won't come.
So, I'm thinking.
Thinking that there is a sort of freedom and there's justice and there's equality
In stagnation
A cleverly orchestrated, delusionary imitation.
All covetousness colored in the collusion of useless demonstration
Like the Black Lives Matter, collective masturbation.
FOLLOW ME NOW . . .

May every synapse in your mind be fertilized, then made blind
By this polite, benign, unkind, IDOL, impotent stagnation
Let all stagnate!
Stand still and gather together, one with the other
Go ahead and protest in your collective stagnation, but stagnate just the same
All must stagnate!
Slavery to slavery
Proper absorption of all authority
Every obfuscation
Teach all men to unite and **OBEY**
Every neck to a single leash
Every back under the lash of a collective lie, believed
Collectively, an "ism"
Now, let the keepers of the lash and the holders of the leash give out medals for service
Received reverently from the thieves
Stand still
Sacrifice
Follow orders
Serve
Sacrifice even more
Fester together a while, but remain willing
OBEY!
Call it "NATION BUILDING"
Give no reprieve
The collective is all, and so it is
The imbecile will always smile in order to enjoy this, his unlimited submission
And he needs his entertainment

Stay Human

So, entertain him without limits!
Give him speeches about the good
Teach him to ignore the conditions
Give them all poison for food
Now, sell the poisonous antidote
SIDE NOTE: Now you may approximate fully the life of the living
REDACT THAT: Man's soul must be emptied!
Now, indoctrinate the Christians
Let him have his religion
But regulate both his charity and forgiveness
'The world of the future' is now another meaningless quote
Everything that refuses to be ruled, sold, or controlled, must go
Break every soul!
The souls must be broken!
Kill man's aspirations
Tokenize his integrity
Turn truth into mere credibility
Massage his guilt
Make him feel small, surely he'll wilt
Quantify all bereavement prudently in brevity
Ensure him that PeAceBstill
And then . . .
Keep him moving and working and **CONSUMING** and dying
Make him uncertain, unclean, unkept, and inept
But never deny the conception of greatness
Kill it from within
Great men will not be ruled!
We must have no great men
The great is the rare, the difficult, the creative, the caring
Confound this greatness in mummies' womb
Take it
This greatness
Abort it
Smother it in comparison
In competition
Any impetuous toward improvement must be dominated demurely
Bring forth shrines of frightened men
Enshrine them!
And then surely . . .
Those pontificating preachers and greedy leaders
For those that practice sorcery and "believe" that they are healers

June Barefield

For the litigator and the judge, the useful idiots, bankers
For The Generals with the guns
Give to these, a sense of entitlement
Entitle them!
Wrap them up in vain submission
Teach them early on that this is love
Set him apart
Now above
Give to him purpose
These frightened men
Raise them up
Enshrine them
In stagnation!

All MUST stagnate
I think.
THINK, I'll take a nap.
Now that I've thought it over a bit
I'm thinking stagnation's just a trap
MEN MUST ACT
Ya think?
THINK LOUDER NOW.

Stay Human

Photograph

I pray for the world
But the world ain't mine
Wish I could change the world
But I can only rarely change my own mind
Wavering as it does from who i am to what i was
Favoring the latter in matters of this world just because
Because of the conditioning
The planned obsolescence
This obsession with obsessing
Total acquiescence to every mandate given by The State
And so I pray
I do
And then I meditate thinking on these things
Whatever is true and pure and kind and lovely
Humbly, I pray
Take a good look inside
But the world ain't mine
I was given this
Livin' in this
Trap
Wish I could save the world, but I can't save my damn self
In fact, all of the pieces of me at peace with me are jagged and frayed at the edges
Puzzle pieces that don't fit
Sharply formulated, a mechanism used for survival through all the fazes
. . . of my life
Stages where I ignored all of the writing on the wall
But the one thing that I always knew
Intuitively, I knew that this thing we all call living is a con . . .
A witches' brew, boiled and stirred from birth
The soul of man, being systematically unearthed
Wrapped up in the rhetorical, historical fantasy, giving credence to a curse
"The world"
Given graciously to the goaded
The desperate classes
The masses of the people not unlike myself
Unlearned, even with the trappings provided by your Ivory Tower Academia
Controlled, lingering underneath a canopy, created for the proverbial ends to justify

June Barefield

The all compliant means
The world is all greed
At every level
I contemplate, imagining the ignorance, and the bliss
Of yesterday
With bated breath
Obsessed with the knowledge that something has been set in place
So, I pray for the world drifting inside the doldrums everyday
Day by day
And these days, nothing proposed will last for more than a day anyway
So, fuck what them say!
Spend my time watching what they do
Words have no meaning
The project is for a new ameri**K**an century
Aquarius, the age
All memory must fade into this artificial reality, where sufferers are smitten
Written cleverly out of the life equation, tethered to the machine, "believing"
False information
Under the charming spell of snakes, all bound to the corporation
So, I pray for the world
But the world is not mine
I was given this
Living in this
Trap,
An open-air prison
But "He has risen," says the overly civilized Christian
Overtly committed
Inwardly smitten
It's all been written
Seems nobody's reading
Britain, the beast
Amerika, the wicked
The **invention** of the so-called Jew, conversely, has been hidden
And to think your own thoughts in a so-called democracy, forbidden
So, I pray for the world
That Man never came here to bring peace, but a sword
So, here it is
And in-between dreams, I can see spots of time
Where a gigantic snake is shedding its skin
Billions comply

Stay Human

Bow down and praise the lie
Every principality and power, lined up with the mental
Spiritual wickedness, in high places
Nothing anywhere is accidental
And no-thing is sacred
Millions die
And now, deprivation is life
But not just in the *3rd World*
Now you, *You's a nigga too!*
So, now, the shoe is on the other foot, and that foot is up your ass!
Pray for the world tho'
"Give God the wheel"
Take a photograph!

June Barefield

Selah

I have nothing.
Seems I've run clean out of ransom money for your little rescue, Bitch
I can't save you!
Won't try
Sold my cape many years ago, I don't fly!
Thought I loved you at one time, finally realized, your eyes lie
From time to time, I think on all the time I wasted, but not for lack of trying
For everything under the sun, I'm told, there is a time
I never could quite say the words goodbye
It's due time!
Perhaps you thought me broken, but you cannot kill a beautiful weed, Bitch
We don't die!
Come to realize in life loneliness does apply, sometimes
Now clearly, I see this web I've spun, and still, I smile
So, whatever remains of my spirit, I measure out now in bits and pieces
Every fear of a natural order, complete with an understanding of who I've become
Come what may
The roulette table of my life dictates my next gamble each day
I amble toward the reawakening of the light I lost yesterday, trying to participate
And what an absolute mess I made
To be granted such grace, and lifted up out of this place, created out of my own ignorance
Pledging my allegiance to hate
Thinking my actions bonafide in a righteous sort of way
My Rage Against This Machine turned out to be a terrible miscalculation of my own fate
Trying to play the life game, but the wrong way
A reckless definition of love
& Defiance
My environment, and example of love
Our ultimate union, considering these factors
And the pageantry of it all
It wore off quickly, didn't it?
So, it's all a matter of forgiveness and growth
To be human is to learn the lesson of love and to suffer until we know
So, I love you today as never before
Today, I know
To have nothing is more than I need.
Thank you for the lesson, Katherine Lynn.

Selah.

Stay Human

936

I know that people are persons, and that persons are human
Right?
I mean, we all shit and piss and fart and fuck
And we all gotta eat
Right?
Human as we are, I often wonder about the "being"
The part about elevated insight and transcending out of the darkness of our personhood
Into the kindness of daylight
The "being" part
Right?
Everybody knows that people are persons, and that persons are human
Right?
I mean, we've all gotta fight to survive, negotiate with the hive mind, we all gotta try
Right?
We all lie and cheat and steal, and connive, justify every lie, striving for a better way
Thinking this the only way, feeling a certain kind of way, merely existing
From day to day
Unable to just **be** alive
Right?
"Being" alive isn't enough, ever
So, we collect stuff
Taught the comparison narrative at public school, but never the importance of love
I know though
People are just persons, huh?
To be human in a world of Publik Figures!
I can't figure out who's more ignorant, the public, or the nigga out here, selling a bluff
Considering people are persons and just being human is enough!
It's the "being" part we got all fucked up
Right?

June Barefield

KaLeB Flow

Everything iz war
War on drugs, thugs, smiles and hugs
War on crime.
I am a criminal.
Black.
Subliminal
War for oil, water, land, resource
Rejoicing while parroting the line
"Terrorism" sublime
False flags, flown in time by elected officials who propagandize the times
Time after time.
War for peace
War for the young mind
Mimes on both sides for sale
Created **WAR** machines endure
More war to explore in lands where I am sent away to fight
I am poor
And 4 me
Everything iz WAR.
I am the 99 percent
Born pure.

Stay Human

Professional Negro

Track and trace genocide
Encoded genetic time torture vibes
Machiavelli, the prince mindstate for mistaken identity crimes
A Deboise debutant
Admission device
Babel alive
So, dead men contrive
Catastrophy, generationally normalized
The "who am i"-summation toast
In suit and tie
"All rise!"
Now, pour the wine
A post-traumatic slavery syndrome compromise
Screaming "Free at Last!"
At critical mass, an image control pass
So, now you pass nigga
You are them
Eureason, nigga?
A succession of survivalist strategies concerning peace
Another Greek Negro-wannabe
Another Professional all Negro coalition hero
Raised up on the line
Masonic tradition,
European friendly; so, everything is contrition
Close your eyes now
Bow your heads down
Recite after me:
"Our Father who art in heaven, hallowed be thy name . . ."
Unsound insight on a shadow plane time flight
A "Professional" Nigga
Black face, White brain
On Hamilton Terrace, mastering the mystery of this misery for "progress"
For context
A contest, suggesting excellence
An embellishment development
Menticide
On Hamilton Terrace
Close your eyes now
Bow your heads down
Recite after me: . . . **"Negro, please!"**

A Longing

Not yet in love
But always in love
With love
Forever falling
In and then out
Of love
For the mere wanting
A longing to love
A pure, UN-fade-able
Faithful, sincere, unfailing
GRATEFUL LOVE
Instead, misled
Bonded momentarily for insignificant moments of lustful loves
Talking high-sounding; oh, so temporary nonsense!
Pretending, then attempting to convince myself into something else
That is **not** Love
Trapped.
Ensnared in fragmented snares, unprepared and unaware
Playing truth or dare with a lie
In the blind eye of my mind, unable to intuit
What's felt so deep down inside
Knowing
REASONABLE CANNOT LOVE FIND!
Trifling down roads
Dallying dalliance upon dalliance
Discovering and then
Rediscovering
Uncovering the truest truth, denied
Not yet in love
I re-enter my depths
Intense
I reflect
Intent to find this love
A longing.

Life Dance

This merry dance is death
From birth.
We dance this dance with every breath.
Every step we barter
Bandaged & battered.
Scarecrows & scallywags, stranded
Straddling something hidden and forbidden
Singing this death song from the beginning
Inborn, subtle & ongoing
Smitten on edge, 'til end
Conscious, yet unknowing
Glowing underneath this placid singleness
Where the ignorance of our agitation shivers intently
Together with a patient, watchful remembrance
Superbly savage & magnificent
A sort of choice in nightmares
A reverence
Watched over by the stars.
This merry dance of death in life, reflecting in our faces
Lined, wrinkled & shrinking
Marked by toil & deception
In success & love for life's glorious emancipation.
Dancing this dance towards death
. . . for life.

Citizen

Divergence
Never wholly forceful.
Accept banality
A tantalizing torture
Then gradual vague submission.
Accept it
Between here and there for now
Where a very low sort of gold mist hovers above the tide marks
But one may hope between the lines
Always between the lines
Hoping and
Quietly dreaming
Between the lines
Believing upon opal gonads in organdy
Depending on eternity
An afterlife after life
Between here and there for now.
Sunflowers, born in the wind
Planted in the crags
A fearful normalcy symptomatic of this condition.
Accept it.
The forever and ever contradiction
A descriptive edict of indecision
Wholly prescribed and completely Christian
That white baby Christ Jesus predilection
Disguised in abstraction
An "ism"
The citizen's assimilation
An asylum
"ATTENTION, WAL-MART SHOPPERS!"
Anecdotal
Celebratory
A dysfunctional vegetable bin.
Accept banality, hoping between the lines
Always, between the lines . . .
Esthetics, sold separately.
Accept it
Citizen.

Stay Human

"[The State] is an institution run by gangs of murderers, plunderers, and thieves, surrounded by willing executioners, propagandists, sycophants, crooks, liars, clowns, charlatans, dupes, and useful idiots —an institution that dirties and taints everything it touches."

Hans-Hermann Hoppe (b. 1949)

German-American academic

Fish

The "Nation," LIKE THE "STATE," is a conceptual, subjective, abstraction personified . . . .

The state, outside of itself, has no life of its own---apart from the individual. All life is individual life. The individual is bound to "The State" through collectivist thinking, manufactured by those that control you. It is our collective, indoctrinated thought, our participation as individuals that bring the concept of "Nation" into existence . . . the individual, now merely a victim. The individual has always been a victim, twisted against himself to this alleged higher power called "emperor," "king," or "society," or "nation," or "race," or "THE STATE." Collectively, a thought-"ism." Mind prison. Together, one mind, imprisoned.

A very strange sort of paradoxical concoction of errors is represented as truth. Thinking thoughts, manufactured by the machine. Doctrinal, historical, and collectivist systems, The State, accepted and represented as benevolence and "love" for humankind. Call it now 'tradition,' or 'culture,' or 'education,' or simply call it what it is: **Institutional mind control**.

I am told that under the sun, there is nothing new; from the first human sacrifice made for the good of the tribe to the heretics burned at the stake for the glory of "God" to the millions enslaved and exterminated in the name of a superior race ideology. The same collectivist immorality has served to justify every atrocity ever, past or present. There is no right or wrong: **it is thinking that which makes it so.** Human thought has been, and remains to be, processed for ownership. Hook, line, and sinker. Who is it though, this fisher of men? Think about it: Who owns your soul?

Stay Human

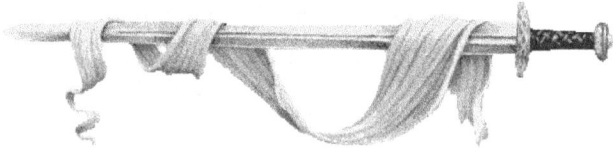

"Violence is man re-creating himself."

Frantz Fanon (1925-1961)

French Afro-Caribbean psychiatrist and political philosopher

June Barefield

Upside Down

When your right side's up, but forced to live inside out
    because everything is upside down,
Fumbling about with tarnished crowns and meaningless things
Turned around
Beyond the point, in a place you no longer wish to go
To be
Upside down, staring into the abyss that has become humanity
A vision of me
An abominable inversion of reality
Tuned into a frequency, provided to you by system clowns
Upside down,
Teaching children about the "correct" pronouns
And the height X the width is equivalent to a cumbersome circumference, tabulated
    by those in authority, the "System" clowns
The majority made the minority,
Molded cleverly into a sickening conformity
That is, until ideas become action
When the ideal transaction is merely a transfer of peace
One to another
All over the world,
When spirit and matter are one
All over the world
Inside he who would for she who will because of those who did
Sacrifice to live, to struggle, not merely exist
Consider this: INTERCONNECTEDNESS
All over the world
When ideas become action in alignment with exacted conditions for the acceleration
    of brand new expeditions
And so, we must explore until the EXPLOSION of vision,
Collectively
All over the world
Solid and fixed,
. . . this
Interconnectedness.
Let it be
And so it is . . .
It must be.

Stay Human

Demon

Water iz life.
So, we sell it to you
Make you pay for it
While we pollute it.
Then, what must we do?
We must charge you a fee, because it now must be
Cleansed & filtered
Again and again.
A civilized trend for civilized men.

Food is free
But we make you pay to hunt& fish& farm& grow whatever you need to eat.
We are, all of us, criminals for the crimes we have committed
But we connive.
So, you run out and vote for whomever we promote as u peck out a living, poking
    and pecking about
    Human chikens

You devote your life to our enterprise of greed.
We pay you a wage, sit back and watch as you dig your graves, chasing your tails in
    concentric waves
    Servants of "free" trade
Convinced of this lie, your consumptions multiply **X3**
So, Y try realizing a new lie, accepted as the old truth?

U die
Unjustified,
Tied to the ball and the chain that you bought in life.
And now?

Now, we sell this same fib so that your children may live just as you did,
Chained to a wage,
A slave.

This is your freedom.
A demon.

"First, *we overlook evil. Then we permit evil. Then we legalize evil. Then we promote evil. Then we celebrate evil. Then we persecute those who still call it evil.*"

Fr. Dwight Longenecker (b. 1956)

American parish priest

Stay Human

Another Un-poetiK Rant

The seductive presumptive function of the "world" is that one conforms
To ultimately obey, falling backward into an age where technology is an incurably cosmodemonic mindfuck
Stipulated in syncopation by the status quo that humanity be stuck, that this mindfuck be ever present and relentless
Spending energy on dis-logic
Distraction
Disharmony
& Discontent
Divided,
Bent on the destruction of *one's* circadian cycle
Disrupting any likeness of the Christ
Trifled with to remain unfit, consenting
Trending in epidemic proportions where genuinely a credible lie will suffice
Any sort of plausible deniability is considered twice as nice.
The only thing authentic in ameriKa is "the lie"
The mass consumption of said lie
The manipulation and multiplication of The "People of the Lie"
Hence, the hive mind
Herd mentalities together contrive
Intertwined cleverly with some artificial cloud in the sky.
Dead or alive
Every imagination reimagined into vice
A computer love virtual device, derived dastardly to oversee the derision
A functional fracturing of any compunction that is to rely upon truth:
One must comply!
Conformity, complex completion for societal norms
Comfortable and warm
Lonely, but cozy and obediently reformed
Only the phony slowly grow into the ever-present, all knowing EYE
And one must comply!
Confined to the process of thought, manufactured for you by the machine
    confirming each un-truth amicably through some unknowable kinesis
    creating amnesia amongst the blind
Casted lines by these "fishers of men" into a realm, dreadfully transformational.
And you'd best comply!
Take for instance, the hubbub them call 'the legal disputation'
Merely another transaction for the desperate peasant, lacking direction

June Barefield

An infection, injected like them Covid experiments
More like extortion retorted backwards walking a crooked line forward, drawn by the all-knowing, prying eye in conspiratorial times for compliant minds, exacted for the mimes to mine
Educated morons, all comply
Tryna balance what u do with who you are
Every complexion, colored with the language of politiK
A systematized indoctrination covet.
Just look outside!
The consistent tone is just so obvious.
Seriously, really; take a look, human beings are oblivious, and being systematically slaughtered
The institutional mind hacks control for the capturing of every soul
Where stagnant placation is presumably freedom
Slavery now, en vogue
In the same sort of web, made by the spider to entrap the fly
The succubus in silk, consummating control of the mind
Where the iron is tricked in order to subdue the wood
From university to university with adverse certainty
The pathology of the über-rich, the so called "elite"
A psychopathy, enriching every art, and all the so-called "sciences" producing a billion buffoonish appliances
   silencing every real thing
And people are just patients, indulging in make-believe
So, whatever is true or pure or worthy, gets quietly erased
In the land of articulate tricks.
Artificial artifacts perform linguistic gymnastics
A systematized indoctrination covet
A seductive presumptive function.
Even mathematics is a lie:
So, 2+2=5!
And there aren't any
Ancient recipes to serve over my **INSTANT** rice!
The natural act of truth has been banned
And our so-called superstructure is being demolished, purposefully, with a smile
Death by 1000 cuts.
The tipping point
A head gut-invocation
Consecrated with contemptible sameness.
The story is the story of the egoistic mind, drawing you to emote inherited human pain
Mixed together with the toxicity of a vain but glorious assumption

Stay Human

Assuming that this inherited human pain is real.
If it even exists
Each reaction is masked in an abstraction to contradict
Made out to be reality
Perceived
Presumably as a
Non-productive, seductive function.
So, you had best just comply, citizen!

"Unfortunately, there can be no doubt that man is, on the whole, less good than he imagines himself or wants to be. Everyone carries a shadow, and the less it is embodied in the individual's conscious life, the blacker and denser it is."

Carl Gustav Jung (1875-1961)

Swiss psychiatrist, psychotherapist, psychologist, and pioneering evolutionary theorist

Stay Human

Human Animal

Sons of God
Daughters of Men
Doctors in the morning
Lawyers in the afternoon
Upside down in handcuffs
Silently consenting to this lamentation of fear
In the same web, made by the spider to entrap the fly
Where the iron is tricked in order to subdue the wood
And silver, gold, and every precious metal must be tried by fire and refined
But the argument that explains everything
Explains nothing at all
Servile fatalistic ideas, an inculcation
An indication of the possibility of validation
Indicating one's placement
Castrated before this mysterious altar of power
Of principality
The dominated spirit
Devoured
In the unreality
By the unnatural
Exploited in a calculated fashion
Systematically cast by classes
An extraordinary rendition of "infinite justice,"
Empowered 2b radical in its eviL
So eviL, in fact, that this empowerment is validated by the people
But in the end
Only destruction can function
Committed to hatred and to cruelty
That eviL will become suicidal
Destroying itself;
The powerful ones, fearful ones
The roving sons, dead ones
All
Giants amongst giants
All
Fallen.

June Barefield

The Future

It belongs to machines and the zombified robots who operate them without compassion
    or empathy for human beings
You are being unnaturally selected
Infected with the notability of the lie
An apathetic populace, tuned in to state-sponsored news agencies, owned by billionaires
    negative polarity, pulsating and made popular
        ocular extortion, coerced until violence becomes a remedy, accepted willingly
Blue lives matter, nigga!
Conflate the lie now!
Obfuscate the delusional citizenry on a left-brained sort of symmetry!
No synergy.
Correspondence, unbalanced, sickening the energy
The legality of man-made authority
Smiles wide, imbued with a Crocodilian guile
    ORDER IN THE KOURT!
Frequency, tuned all the way down.
There's but **WHITE NOISE NOW.**
Frequent energy, synchronized and completely callous in every house from town to town.
    AmeriKan Pie all around!
Must be whatever's in the water
Perhaps the chemical spray in the air
Or the poisonous immunizations, created to further thin out the herd
Combined with toxic sources of food, modified genetically to keep you sickly.
    Willingly, we pay for heart disease, hypertension, and diabetes;
        then we pay the pharmacy.
The doctor takes his cut from the prescription; insurance for your "health," the remedy.
Population, lethargic, inert, and lazy.
    FREEDOM IS SLAVERY.
The institutions you should trust, in reality, are the enemy.
TOO **COMFORTABLE** TO B ANGRY
In ameriKa.
All sheep to the slaughter, tip toeing in shallow, polluted waters, subservient, made frantic
    and afraid.
This exact fear, obediently passed down and adopted by the sons and daughters of SLAVES.
    Comfortable, willing slaves!
        White ones, black ones, brown, red and yellow slaves, living paycheck to paycheck
            without realizing they're slaves!
This, the home of the brave.

Stay Human

Now, stand the fuck up, nigger, the national anthem's being played
    wound around your mind like the spider's silk.
      "Thank you for your service."
Milked like the poison dripping off of the factory-raised cows' tit$
Or that chicken they create from incubation to your plate at home in less than 8wks.
Methuselah by the time you're 40, because you can't get off meat.
So enthralled that you cannot move.
You do not wish to move.
      Television, twisted, transfixing this sickness, piercing the skin, entering the
        bloodstream, encapsulating what it is you think.
Now you won't think at all.
Not for yourself.
Just a replaceable cog on a wheel, created for the machine
    THE MACHINE!
No empathy at all 4 human beings.

Endemic

A cheerful ignorance
Formulated from an affable innocence
A darling sort of degradation
A period of training and preparation
And gradually, cohesion
Singing the star-spangled banner.
Hand over heart, pledging allegiance . . .
Absolutely tragic
Strategically dumbed down
12 years of "schooling."
The penitentiary is college
A tragic masquerade.
The ameri**K**an negro, still in chains
Greek negros boast Alpha, Phi, Sigma, Beta, whatever . . .
Systematically, them turn Grey
Not so much educated
. . . but trained
What to think, believe, consume and follow.
This, the created chaos of existence
Generationally endemic
Cheerfully ignorant.

Negrotudes

Nigga negrotudes . . .
Nigger boy, colored gurl
U, afro-american U
These negrotudes, piercing opaque prostration with too much patience
Eager to debate the state of the ameri**K**an negro today
Quoting Dr. King
Still waiting on freedom to ring.
No black past.
No future.
Only now remains.
These negros
A white destiny
And their negrotudes . . .
Nigger boy, colored gurl
U, afro-american U . . .
A mechanism
Pieced together w/o realism.

2099

No need for genius.
Genius is dead.
Life's played out on an artificial stage.
Them peoples eradicate any note of genius by the 6th grade
And I'm afraid
Afraid that in 2099, a lil boy will die with the same scars as me
Digging in the dark underneath artificial stars
Nothing but instinct to cling to
Aptitude anger
Another young Willie Bosket
A stranger
In a strange world,
Stuck dealing with the truth of fiction
The truth, an emotional reflection, without refraction
Understanding only retribution
An interdiction, built on illusion
Educated by patients
Digested, assimilated, taken into the rigidness of existence
Infected early on to be institute property
The psychoanalyst, they have traced this poison back to the womb
Civilized properly

No need for genius
A young Willie Bosket prophecy
Underneath artificial stars
Dealing with the truth of fiction
2099 . . .
Lil boy,
Same scars.

Stay Human

How?

Young and black, and I'm innocent
But I'm ignorant
Synonymous
One and the same without proper revelation
Sensational historical fantasy, I embrace as my own, "believing" them facts
Grown now
Learned to investigate my own now
Refusing any proposition or proposal providing inconclusive solutions for the innocent
Ignorant, now
Somehow the ignorance just deepens now
The more I learn, the less I know
Look into my eyes now
How to make a lasting change
Rearrange the patterns of poverty and prejudice now?
How?

June Barefield

Namesake

Suspicious must be me
My Daddy, he named me after he
But "Suspicious" has got to be my name
Everywhere I go
No one will admit it
But I see it just the same
My name
I feel it
Sense it
Everywhere, all the time
Everyone in line
My life
And that suspicious eYe
I surmise that it is I
At least in my mind
The usual suspect, unusually subject to suspicion
Daddy's baby boy
Mother's priceless child
Pretty much, it's black and it's white
Suspicious
That's me
Suspicious
That's why.

Stay Human

"Settle your quarrels, come together, understand the reality of our situation, understand that fascism is already here, that people are dying who could be saved, that generations more will live poor, butchered, half-lives if you fail to act. Do what must be done, discover your humanity and your love in revolution."

George Lester Jackson (1941-1971)

American author, revolutionary, and prisoner

June Barefield

Bourgeoisie Negro

They act surprised, intoxicated by the lie of white life, thinking white thoughts, taught to compromise, trained and educated to obey. Obedient negros are basically compliance officers for the masses of their people. They're afforded great comfort in most instances and are very influential in molding the process of thought that the lower socioeconomic class of negros cling to. This bourgeoisie negro is made out to be some sort of hero. For the most part, he is worshipped and looked upon as some sort of leader. Always in political cadence, and often occupying significant positions in government because they are loyal first and foremost, to The State.

Whatever is purported as a "Civil Liberty" is merely the act of kicking the can of oppression and domination down the road. A fucking fraud, perpetrated by these manufactured, user-friendly Negros, crying out for peace, hollering about a dream, playing make-believe. These Negros see only what they are told to see. What sickens me personally is that this educated fool *believes*. He has been so indoctrinated into this culture of thieving elites, and the actor-appointed politikal class of criminals, he *believes*. He thinks that he can rearrange the Master's house by using the Master's tools. I'd like to think that this bourgeiosie negro is unaware of the fact that he, himself, is only a tool. A constant advocate for peace, democracy, and the "rule of law."

There are politicians and judges and intellectuals and theologians and lawyers and entertainers and athletes and preachers. These niggas here are even philanthropic when it serves them, each one captured and convinced of the All AmeriKan lie, comfortable and proud. They're successful in persuading the masses of the people time and again to be law-abiding, and peaceful. The day is quickly approaching when the common man must wake up and recreate himself, or remain under attack from every institution that exists here in our fair ameriKa, where these willing black sycophants help to enable continued fascism, and the murderous treatment of their own people. Please do not get it fucked up! It is this "talented ten percent" negro who turns cheeks and barters deals within a system of white, racist supremacy.

"Them!" Who are placed out in front as spokesmen and spokeswomen time and again, eager to polish the Master's crown of barbarism and savagery, then politely call it 'democracy.' And if one is not paying close enough attention to history, admiration for these educated, so-called leaders and heroes of ours becomes automatically baked into what we're trained to think the truth is. Do not be deceived.

AmeriKa was built on racism and hate. And while the majority fights and scratches to survive, it is this bourgeoisie nigga that infuriates me most of all. He is so proudly despicable; in my eyes, an abomination. This bourgeiosie nigga now legitimizes, absolves, and actively participates in the neverending cultivation of this police state fascism, complicit in every crime. Pride cometh before the fall! So, do not act surprised, thinking that since you've learned to behave just like your masters that you will be pardoned. I do not believe that your masters can save you in the end. You are merely the tool used to control me. For now, you are 'them,' but soon enough, when you are no longer useful, the Master will cast you aside. And on that day, nigga, do not act surprised.

June Barefield

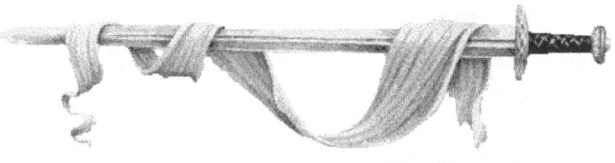

"Most people have to, at some time or another, stand alone and suffer. Their final shape is determined by the response to their probation. They emerge either as slaves of circumstance, or in some sense, as captains of their souls."

Charles E. Raven (1885-1964)

English theologian and Anglican priest

Stay Human

Wind

Phrases unfold to form columns in intervals
Words become images
Like individuals dressed to the right when marching
Every eye right on the left
Another day, sunset; another step
Another breath, inhaled, exhaled, becoming one concentrated mindstate
All following in the footsteps of the inept
Quiet is kept
A slow march, and then, a sudden death
And to contemplate one's own steps, made to appear an increasingly risky bet
Follow me now . . .

Rest for the wicked comes the same as for the wise
Disaffected and downtrodden, just look into my eyes!
Another convict of confliction, addicted to distraction, seething inside, convinced of destruction
Now dis-con-nec-ted in jest for the jester
A seed, infested with a poisonous nectar
To experience the same environment in each and every sector
But remain separate
To ENTER the CENTER, dismembered
To remember the coldest winter ever, clearly
For the dearly departed, and the eerily undone
Sons of the morningstar, bar-none
On earth, as it is in heaven
Conceptual complexities
For an abnormal reality
And still, the wind that blows is all that anyone, anywhere, really ever knows
Everyday reality is life and death; but the reality, not everybody knows
So, not everybody grows
But the wind still blows
Thru the towns and the cities, I go
With a dream, built on brutality, inconsistent and unheavenly
    until seventy times seven is seen, tethered heavenly
But not in me
Unwilling am I to take fees from fleas, or cop pleas for early release
My time and my crime are all of me

June Barefield

Warehoused now
A commodity for BIG Business, and prison is the industry
So, I learned the mind of many men
The distance in reality between them and me
The reality of illusion
The beauty inside delusion
All pinned hopes and pen stripes on pen blocks through dark nights
From lowdown to upright
Confirming insight is paradise
    . . . of mind
A seed, planted and groomed to verify the facts, and observe only the facts
The antagonist, along with his foolishness, will remain blind; stars will shine, but for Jupiter the malcontent—his prison will remain to be
    . . . his mind
So, every act remains impure when packaged with ill-intent
And misconception feeds deception, the perceptive know this
Indeed
I don't think they will ever be quite capable of killing off a beautiful weed
As long as there's a seed left to sow
Now I see, but the wind still blows
The wind
All I will ever really know.

No Reprieve

I saw the poor in a putrid, filthy pile of flesh, dying in the doorway of what religion has
    left for us
Trained to "believe"
To the young is preached this holy doctrine of work
And at rock bottom, this is nothing but the politi**K** of inertia
Everything for tomorrow
Heaven or Hell
An afterlife after life
But to consider your soul today
In the here, for the right now
To open that door
To take that one blind leap into the realization of what is
To truly trust this faith and live
To discover the truth of what really is will never be . . .

Your God is your stomach.

Your religion, blasphemy.

And tomorrow never comes
The afterlife after life dies too
Bound up with us.
A putrid, filthy pile of flesh
In the doorway
In the doorway of what religion has left for us
Dying.

Who Is "They"?

Them
The crocodile people
Villainous and despicable
But unexposed
Hand-hidden
The same hand that controls the politician
Boniface
The 1 un-Holy one
"Them"
Each and every road must lead back to Rome.
Just pull back the curtain
"There they go!"
In the pulpit
Pontificating at your Statehouse
In the kapitals
On the kongress floor
In the boardrooms at Blackrock
The WHO
Bilderberg
The WEF
Gathering together at the Tavistock Institute
University at Chicago
Everywhere, exerting control
"Them" . . .
The crocodile people.

Dark Matter

Unum Sanctum
Mankind's curse
The corporation
Of The Apostle Peter
To capture the Soul
Of man
The landlord
Of a Nation Consecrated
Deeded to the house of the unholy 1
Where every road is laid
To Rome
The world of the dead
And the Beast.

A cemetery
Mankind's curse
The Roman road
Boniface and
The Papestry
Unum Sanctum
Mankind's curse.

June Barefield

"A man perceptible by the spirit of revolt under one or more of its forms,- opposition, investigation, criticism, innovation, endowed with a strong love of liberty, egoistic or individualistic, and possessed of great curiosity, a keen desire to know. These traits are supplemented by an ardent love of others, a highly developed moral sensitiveness, a profound sentiment of justice, and imbued with military zeal."

Emma Goldman (1869-1940)

Lithuanian anarchist, revolutionary, political activist, and writer

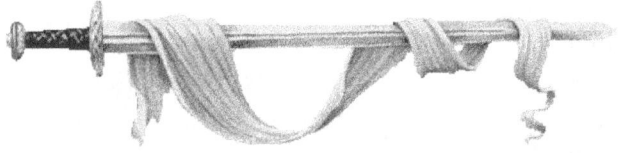

Stay Human

Premonition

I haven't any needs.
None.
A man with no past
No future.
Never another moment like *Now*.
I am, have been, will remain
Sutured up by my experience
Another experiment
But Now
I am unconcerned with your likes or dislikes.
My stance is upright.
I don't have to look inside my vest pocket to locate my souL.
It is always there, always near
Bumping up against my ribs, swelling and inflating together with this song I have to give.
Whatever the Lord is, I am strong in He (or She, or It, or Them).
This **energy** is me.
And I am you
And we are ONE
Beyond the optimism of our peasantry, the pessimism of this treachery
This continual oscillation between extremes.
For soon enough, the full flavor of emptiness we must consume
Because . . .
Life is passing away.
The time for charming snakes is over.

I am sadly dazzled by the glorious collapse of the world.
I can see ameri**K**a. She is spreading disaster.
I see ameri**K**a as an ugly curse upon the world
And I can see a very long night settling in.
I see the world and its people being poisoned at the roots, withering and uncouth
The result of inexplicable forces, commanding chaos and disorder
Hiding in the shadows, wading through the shallows
Spiraling down this path where death speaks, and a progress deferred creeps, bottling up
    every avenue of escape; until, we must feel one another belly to belly, without hope
Like grains of sand underneath the ruins at Athens
Like newly discovered pathogens, awaiting fresh patents, lacking nothing at all but
    humanity

June Barefield

Perhaps ... if I became unintelligible, I would be understood immediately.
A hideousness has always lived right between the curse and the gift
And only killers extract from life what they've put into it.

I have a premonition of the end of this.
I can see spots of time where realities have been written.
A cadaver sheds its skin, and sufferers are smitten.
A sort of sieve through which **Anarchy** must be strained
Life (humanity) is passing away.

Never another moment like Now; so, each moment is innocence.
Technology is only mental.
Without wisdom, there is no language for the heart; so, man's spirit is eaten.
The human body is out of tune, out of sync with Mother Earth.
One way or another, we must return to **Her** (Earth).

Infected

This goes out to the hovering hoards
    and to the drovers driving the shameless swarms:
Be forewarned
Losing your selves, trying to figure out which "self" to be
With so many options, distractions, and deflections, misdirections, and misguided
    bastardized so-called insurrections
Just infected
Ordered for an illustration of life
Taken up into and underneath the subsumption of what next to choose
What next to believe
In-between imperceptible crevices
Tight-roping on slender threads
Scaling iffy cliffs, and eviscerated ledges
Hedging debt like a risky bet, lost friday night at the fight
Dealt a diabolical, rascally dreamer's hand
Playing the Life Game on knees and hand
A fool's game without a plan
With fool's gold
& Greed
For markets
& War
For targets . . .
But only poor boys and girls for the fodder
And always imitating the aristocrat
The diplomat, the autocrat, and of course, the new celebrity brat
Praying to God with the devil's soul
Interloping on the bottom floor for more and more
Always wanting more
Forsworn like foreign oil
Always this seduction for more
In droves, driven by the drovers, driving the swarms
Losing yourself, choosing which "self" to be.
B 4 warned
Mischief-maker!
Persona non Grata!
B 4 warned!
This goes out to the hovering hoards, the drovers, driving the shameless swarms.

June Barefield

A Witness

There is no mood, exactly a lavender lady
Calendar babies
Minds occupied mostly by carnival lights and almost maybes
Craving an ancient recipe, served over this instant rice
Might I ban the colors of my television tonight?
All the made-up faces
The fake eyes and the perfect thighs
That tummy tuck hologram demise, where every plastic wish is worth more than my next breath, but . . .
I love this life, because
I believe in death.
I know death must be.
The question is, "What the fuck is life?"
I keep a ready eYe on the civilized as they bumble together in a heap of catatonic hysteria, unaware
While the secret of *6iX* thousand years slowly crawls back into being.
The stars have gone crazy, and the Sun is angry.
So, what I need is a witness
This, a wailing wall type predicament.
So, after you've taken them "holy" rituals to that precious fountain, built by your agencies of fear, I witness two terminally ill mental patients as they place bets on the existence of "God."
I find it all very odd.
I try not to think about it, and I'm failing, but I'm weird.
Nothing anywhere has been fair since my first skinned knee.
Cling do I to love.
I envy the innocent child I never was.
So, I demand a witness!

I would like the testimony of
Reagan
Bush
Clinton
And Obama
About the lifeless shadows on the bricks at "Ground Zero,"
An accounting of all the slaughters across the waters, in Iraq
Syria

Stay Human

Palestine
Afrika
Yemen.

I light a blood red candle in my room that's become a coffin.
I talk to God so often that I always soften.
But still, I need a witness
To the infrequent rains
The three-day notice this country gives to the starving
To the pain.
I talk to God in vain about the current of gentle awakening, running underneath the brown
    crust of my skin.
We need a new commandment
A witness to begin again.

A witness
For all the lavender ladies and the calendar babies, crying out for attention and
    twenty-dollar bills, chained to the asphalt believing it's grace
All the little faces looking up to the fake
Beautiful and "believing" soon to be consumed by the same fate, inevitably learning to
    hate
Generations-tamed "thinking" thoughts manufactured by the machine, and then replaced.

I wish to weep, but sorrow is stupid.
I weep anyway.
I talk to God.
I believe He's really a She, an Agnostic that doesn't even know my name.
I talk to Her anyway.
And these days, I look to purchase the book with the ugliest cover.
This is the kindness that I climb into
Like a magical box where I can cut myself in two.
Hopefully, someday, I can come out whole.

The Only "Why"

I am
The darkness
& The light
The storm
The sunshine
The lightning bolt when I strike
I was there
In your laughter
Every single morning after
The reason 4 everything
Inside your pain
Pendulums swing
Enter into joy again
There I am
The same, unchanged
The only why
Everywhere am I
I am in all of it
The reason 4 everything
Do not try to live without me
Choose me now.
I am love.
The only why
Am I.

Xposed

Merely an incomplete sojourner on this "civilized" life path
1 face
No mask
A traveler, searcher
A journeyman, reaching out to this life, a dreamer
Outside something
In the aftermath of nothing
Full of meaningless meanings and tawdry demons, unscrupulous leanings from sentimental heathens
Yet somehow, I remember my sons and daughters, their mothers and fathers
The pure waters and the **DEEP ROOTS**, emoting the dream within me adaptively
I can recall the beauty of my saVagery
It's Mastery and Kingship
The man in me
A kinship
No red pills or blue chips
A friendship
Sacred and endless
Exposed to four fires I face until the sun's eclipse
A quiet darkness and then stillness
It is here, in this space where a delightful sort of desperation confirms my inspired, UN-resigned will to survive
To thrive
Always teeter-tottering
A balancing act between pity and then pride.
I exist for the collective consciousness in all
Inside
From the college to the synagogue and into the Temple am eYe.
It is true.
I AM the kindling for the embers.
Through the ashes and into the fire, I touch the sky, where elemental unfledged pinion's wave and survey all there is that God has made
ENSLAVED AND THEN . . .
Again begin
Raised up by the wind to be betrayed by my friends and lovers
And their friends and others.
This betrayal, I denied over and again, again and again
Right along with some imperfect prefecture

June Barefield

And of course, the perambulations formulated so nicely to fit my own imagined reality
Along with the weary ramblings of my own defective conjecture
Where all is subjective
A complex maze
Another useless lecture
Always unspectacular
And exposed
Merely, an incomplete sojourner on this "civilized" life path
From envy to apathy to pride and then wrath
Through it all
Always
1 face
No mask.
A complex maze, or just another useless lecture
All but spectacular
And "cheap grace" in my eyes
THE IMMORTAL SIN
A porthole into a place I have never been
The antagonist of my every whim
NO BACKWARD
NO FORWARD
Perfection.
Perfection begins again at Life's end.
I AM INDEED
Exactly what my ancestors were in the beginning.
The ORIGINAL.
Always
Re-gilding eagles and globes, and the philosophical aroma arising from this prose
EXPOSED
There are four fires and then . . .
One must face the Sun
Contemplate life and death, growth and hope
Always
EXPOSED.

Stay Human

Sickness

From a lazy, push-button, unencumbered peace
War for the same sort of vile does increase
Backed by a corporate mind control manipulation entity
Ameri**K**a, "the Great" and her media machine
A 24hr cycle of subterfuge and dribble
Locally, nationally, worldwide. They call it "The News"
Choose a side, citizen!
Red or Blue
Elephant or Donkey
Irrelevant embellishments broadcast by trained monkeys
The formation, if you will, of a "world view"
A comfortable cowardly compromise
Where nearly every eye is averted in the name of "progress", for your safety's sake, or for "The Nation's" ultimate success
But the progress, never for the people, but rather The Military Industrial Complex
The State Department
& The DOD
An ill process, prepared for the magnification of the times
THE WAR MACHINE IS ALIVE!

The militarization of worlds right out in the light, where a titillating split occurs, too tantalizing to confess
Addressing the principalities that underscore the powers in learned persuasion, rendering the masses of the peoples all but lame
Tormented and made mostly tame, trained in every case to obey
Give them all just enough bread, and plenty of mindless dumbshit to keep them entertained
Underneath everything, for "the people " is only
Magnificent fear, and a dangerous vanity, false pride, and seething jealousy, tormenting the main frame in a sickly society,
An illness measured out so articulately for this game of make-believe
This corrupted credence and false confidence are prepared for you
This slowly evolving half-shaped resolve, leaving the souls of men, ultimately, in chains
An easily divisible, opaque, synthetic cipher that "allows" men to accept as true, what in truth is only make-believe, but men believe!
All they've got to do is just put it all on TV, and call it, "The News."

To think critically about what the Truth is, they've made that taboo
    ILL.
This particular sickness, call it 'The discovered "happiness" of modern man;

June Barefield

Call it 'The dirty virtue of an audacious, just credible enough, completely dubious plan,' entirely lacking any sort of an ANTITHESIS.
So, in the name of Jesus, bombs drop over Baghdad
Afghanistan
Syria, Yemen, Libya
Sudan, Somalia, Niger
Venezuela
PALESTINE
And soon enough Iran.
The plan is for a brand new AmeriKan Century.
So, the prodigal ROBS his heir, the miser fortifies his lair, mother's and daughters everywhere are slaughtered without mercy, leaving only the the taste of death to linger in the air.
And magnificent fear fills the hearts of men everywhere.

The world is being anesthetized; it is under the power of an evil spell
An ill-fated formula, concocted by smiling-faced fatalists who politik to front a dispossessed dream unachieved, where **War is Peace**.
Whether or not the truth is real, or merely collateral damage management
An invasion
Occupation
An interdiction
Infection,
Like an ill copulation longing to escape the imagination of well-trained apes
Performing tricks for treats that are recontextualized into rights
And right before your eyes!
To imagine this growing regret and powerless disgust, lusted after in the aftermath of hate, yet not despised
The infection connecting us is hate, disguised.

This slowly evolving half-shaped resolve, draped around the necks of slaves, chained together by hate, admired;
A make-believe reality, all of it contrived
This is the sort of ripple that triples underneath the cover of the night, gliding closer atop an unfaithful enigma, of which, there is no escape.
An ill south wind is rising, lightning violently, striking in the East.
Apocalyptic fires feast, consummating the marriage between the whore of Babylon and the Beast
For it has been written:
"That Man never came here to bring peace . . .
But a sword."

Ice Cream

I asked my mother when I was a very small boy if horses could make babies with cows. Just a little mannish child, curious and wild. She laughed at me chidingly. She told me that was a certain impossibility. I wondered why. And then I asked her why she and my father, a Black man, had me, and why that was, and what I was. She told me I was everything. She said that I was everyone. She bought me ice cream. I think that I understand now, Mommy!

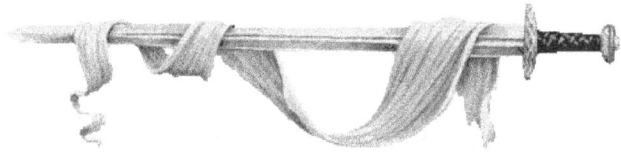

*"We need to do more than just what is right.
We need to join together and right what is wrong."*

Leonard Peltier (b. 1944)

Native American activist and member of the American Indian Movement

Stay Human

Faustian Bargain

I know how you talk,
Using dark humor as you gaze into your black mirror,
    unaware of the darkness inside you.

I know how you talk.
"Pint sized terrorists," the description given for the children you've killed,
Proud of your skills.
It brings to you prominence, importance, cache amongst your komrades.
You cradle your weapon as if it is an extension of your body.
You admire its despicable beauty.
This is who you are,
A killer.

I know how you talk.
"Pint sized terrorists," the description given for the children you've killed,
Numb to the suffering you inflict, surrendering your morality
    to the blind obedience of the military,
Subsumed into the industrial machinery of death.
A very useful idiot are you,
A replaceable cog, colored in the language of politik.

I know how you talk,
Unaware of your own wickedness, following orders
Through the detail of your telescopic lens, the outline
    of another's nose and mouth appear,
Triangulated death.
You hold your breath and gently pull the trigger.
The pink puff of death delivered, as another chest explodes, spinal cord severed.
You exhale, and perhaps contemplate,
In a psychopathic fog that enables you to justify murder again.

I know how you talk.
The interdependence of the lies told to you emboldens this psychosis.
A soldier's cognition, afflicted with this sense of mission,
One of thousands made on an assembly line for death.
You revel in the intimacy of death.

June Barefield

They call you "soldier."
A killer,
Murderer.

I know how you talk.

Stay Human

Beautiful SouL

If I held your hand and then loved you with everything that I am
Would you understand?
Does it even matter
Understanding?
Or is it, this love, that I dream of?
If I walked a thousand lonely miles to see only your smile
Would you know if I told you so?
Innately, would you just know?
Beautiful soul
Would you grow together with me to understand understanding?
Could you sit with me in stillness while everything around us is crashing?
The power of silence in this gigantic world, so demanding.
Beautiful soul
If I held your hand and
Felt your thoughtful mind expand
On this long twisted road
Beyond everything we've been taught
All we believe to know
Would you go to see the spirit of life that radiates in my eyes
Into your souL
Embracing you
With my eyes
Melting inside
Full of life for love's sake
Grateful for the gift of your grace?
If I told you so
Would you believe it so?
Would you long as I do to know a soul
If I held your hand . . .?

Is-ness

Eternal life's a transient
Ephemeral
In us, merely a moment
But purposeful
Perpetual even
A persistent predominance
And all natural.
So, by its very "being," spiritual
This Is-ness
The sacred source of all continuance
Where breath has no return to any point of origin
No recurring ebbs
Only flow
Repeating itself from beauty to heightened beauty
From meaning to even deeper meaning
Genuine essence
Authentic and pure
Eternally life
A forever-presence
Intricately patterned horizontals, diagonals and upright verticals
Every path in alignment, solidified, and centered
A circle
Visions, rich with many colored gems and lovely landscapes that tremble, always
    on the verge of the ultimate revelation
And "it" just is
This Is-ness
Alive with dissonance!
Preciously creating moments
Gaining momentum until pure naked existence
A perpetual flowering, presides
At no time, quivering under the pressure of significance
Completely transient
Inside us all
A Traveling Light
From rose to carnation into the throttling embrace of Euclid
A holy place
Truly

Stay Human

All rendering without depth
Indifferent to time or space
Interested alone with eloquence
With expression
Kindness and fluency
A transient
The meaning and the truth experience
THE BEAUTY WITHIN
This Is-ness
"It"
IT JUST IS.

June Barefield

Another Now

At the fringes inside the fold
The loosening of that exquisite silken rope is known
Life foretold
Where revelation arises in blinding light
Behold
Miraculous signs appear without disguise
Behind the eyes where the shrewdly spectacular arise
RiZeN
Before the fruit was forbidden
Awakened
After the lesson was given
Simplistically gifted
Eons from the civilized, in hues of cinnamon and bronze
At dawn, another **Now** is proposed
With the discipline of a single rose
At the fringes, inside the fold
Ever loosening the silken rope
Behold.

Antithesis

On behalf of the nameless
i am
As He is
In the name of the
Blameless
As IT were, so it shall be
An antithesis, always
As above
So beneath
Unchanged
Like the writings of
Menes
The first man-King
Speaking to the listening silence
Waiting for death
Wondering upon the wind
On behalf of the
Nameless
i am
The inevitable everything
1 breath
Breathing electricity
Everywhere
A Star-High perfection
Clarity connection
The antithesis unchanged
Protected
On behalf of the nameless
Am i

June Barefield

Presence

To touch the stillness
Or perhaps, to live there
In the stillness
All of the time
To disconnect from mind-identity
From ego-hegemony
Tormented in thought
Thinking
All of the time
Unable to find space
Between here and there for Now
Still
To simply B
Still
To watch my thoughts in the presence of **Now**
To touch the stillness and remain somehow
To live, always in the Now
All of the time
In stillness
Inside, forever
Present.

Conflagration Destination
Visions

I was drowsy, half-drunk, downtrodden, and completely divisive
In some sort of stupor
Alone
There came to me this vision about money and privilege and prophecy and remembrance
Where the boule' and the bourgeoisie will get no vengeance
Those who believe that they may simply walk thru' the night crowd and
    endure, protected by their money
The day b4 the apocalypse
There'll be no temperance
Only rain
A torrential rain
And the weather after this day will not change
When all the funny fables and unlearned lessons yield to the metropolis
The day b4 the apocalypse
When every physical force aligns itself with the mental
Colliding with the spirit
To war for your soul
So, go ahead and reach inside your vest-pocket this day and behold the web you weave
The tracks u leave
All of the "temporarily out of order" signs you've written in greed
Segregated this day from any illusion of wholeness
Every delusion of grandeur or attempt at temporary bliss
The day right b4 the apocalypse
On this day, let the murderer and the evangelist
Let them feel one another belly-to-belly without hope
And may every avenue of escape be bottled up on a street-top where flowers don't grow
May the indifference of love be made known in the final hour of man's catastrophe
Severed in silence, synchronized in shadow, smitten and alone to behold
    the sufferers code
On this day
The day b4 the apocalypse
Glance into the abyss
Feel the winds rip and twist
Taste the full flavor of emptiness
When everything sacred or taboo is made meaningless
This day

June Barefield

The day b4 the apocalypse
Your superstructure, **demolished**
Hush the sound of tiptoeing footsteps, creeping slowly with precision into my vision
Come now . . .
Let us walk together thru' the night crowd.

Eclipse

Every day is also night
Now
Hearts pounding
No health insurance
The eminence of war Everywhere
Except for the hearts of the people
Cities collecting roach motels, titty bars, liquor stores, churches, and predatory lending institutes
Drug-addicted victims line the streets, afraid to care
Negro "culture," the vulture eating up the dead
Beware
Them say every brazen scavenger is resolute
The captives are captivated by the spectacle, desperate, and despicable
Small-town business-man devoured
Systematically, demolished with surgical precision
They are *building back better now*
Everything is different Now
Mass deconstruction intensifies division
And Rural ameri**Ka** is quickly becoming nothing but a ghost town
Still, no health insurance
And every day is also night
Now
The bank took granny's house, and then got a bailout
Wall Street bigwigs laugh as the people's tension mounts
Granny worked 50yrs for nothing
Everyday
Her entire life
For nothing
Something wicked this way comes now
The minion's pose is pretense in every photograph
Now
All prose is merely the propaganda that them allow
The law-abiding citizen's head is down
Afraid to breathe in Fauci-town
Granny died alone with nothing
Lately, life is all pain
No pendulum swing

June Barefield

Off-balance alliances compete for the compliant ones
In concert with the inept frequency of a luciferian tune
Everyone moving in syncopation with this wicked rhythm, diagramming
    the disfunction for the next generation
Take a picture!
Because Now
Every Day is also Night.

Void

A depiction of decay in the drab of every thought you have today
Grey strokes, inside the same dead void of yesterday
Every movement less monumental day by day
Any momentum that remains, leading to the grave
An acumen entombment, containment, arrangement,
Lifeless and lackluster, like ameri**K**an cities in decay and ruin
All is decrepit and sickly
The erosion of the paradise that once was the human mind, evicted
Picture the badlands now
The rot and decay from the far edges, slowly inward now
Grey strokes
Deathly afraid of struggle
Every conceptualism conceived for want of relief
To be just comfortable enough to get along
With assurances, of course, but in the end, you'll go along
Transfigured into this being, the eternal "yes!"
You are being transformed, and manipulated, yes?
You own nothing
Not even your own thoughts!
Something about life is becoming more and more decrepit and sickly
Tucked off somewhere in a "15 minute city"
Compacted together feeling so **Smart**
. . . but apart
Like lepers, afraid
A picture of mind-decay
Stuck
In the void
And it's your "thinking" that makes it this way
Our Thinking
On auto, piloted into the in-between
A void
Mind, destroyed
You never mattered and matter even less today
This, the gradual sinking, wasting away
Call it Nothingness deified, sanctified in a very polite salutation
Decay, mind-liquidation
Call it, "Nation being built back better"

June Barefield

A planned destruction destination
With a multitude of degradations
Makes it all so much easier to be controlled
Slowly fading away into the void
. . . of decay
A picture painted to promulgate the weariness of your souL
Whittled down with a purpose for the bartering of your souL
To own what you think in the valley of these dried-up bones
For complete and total **control**
By controllers you'll never even know
Prerequisite measures, perhaps, you'll uncover in the void
Of another life
In a new experience
Somewhere else
Away from here
Remember this void.

liar

the fryer of every uncouth, seemingly smooth angle
wishful thinking in an earthly hell with fallen angels
institute now a chronology to the whole plot
terrestrial time aside
tie all to a chain of reason
reasonable
a cultural delusion
contemporary
conventional
an academic, Ivory Tower subliminal
ruthlessly infused with
Materialism
the philosophy of all present endeavors
devouring the peasant
properly, proclaiming the popularity of the propaganda of the day
enslaved to the pressures of the ordinary
& ordinarily
billions grow gothic erections to the insurrection of the state
& then slowly
them build for themselves their very own estate
ENSLAVED
in the life department
enslaved.

No Respite

We've made an idol out of how democracy is viewed. Our appeasement paints ever so perfectly this skewed observation, deemed a worldwide success story where Capitalism is King. AmeriKa gorges herself, demanding a bounty from every nation. The blood of the young & the poor spills, drenching desert sands in foreign lands, wherein, the interpenetration of this fiction can be facilitated no more. Our collective delusion of this gigantic WHORE, AmeriKa, currently exists, but with an ever-increasing, persistent suspicion. Do not remain suspended in your disbelief. The narrative sold to the people, ripe with the self-importance of over-indulgence and personal greed is beginning to seethe.

     The sun is rising up; the atmosphere, vibrating an electric pulse for truth. This AmeriKan success story has a cost that cannot be paid through the blur and distinction between truth and the fog & falsehood of her ridiculous plausible deniability. The radical off-beat drum of conscience will rise, is rising. It's all been written down.

Follow me now . . .

Stay Human

"If you are unable to find the truth right where you are, where else do you expect to find it?"

Dōgen (1200-1253)

Japanese Zen Buddhist monk, writer, poet, and philosopher

June Barefield

ameriKa

3 days after darkness
marching
destiny manifest, beast shielding always the truth
attempting to rearrange the master's house, using the master's tools
oh, continent of the Un begun, being whom I can barely tolerate
foolish brute
ameriKa.

You ridiculous, awful old space
Babylon
I'll leave my voice here
on the midway at this carnival of lights
I cannot see my face outside of its member
full of gas and splinters
tread upon me not
you of vivid, palpable hatred
congested with synthetically illuminated, forsaken patrons, stripped naked
souls mostly vacant
in ameriKa.

You who persist in me
an endless burning
the master's song
you of impotence, made debonair with rage, encased with diplomacy, disguised as grace
atmosphere, saturated with the futile and frustrated comfortable mummy
shedding the skin of time
when death dawns, you'll leave this place without ever having even your own mind
you national circus of the damned
you murderous system of munitions and inhuman rights
pulsating with greed
passionate about your greed
dismissing every dream but the nightmare
in ameriKa.

You enterprise of criminality that calls me criminal
you who cry out "terrorism" to control the fearful
my pulse-beat wilt not
I forget not the power of silence

Stay Human

in silence, quiet sobs observe the stolen land, wrapped in feces, adorned with silk
every brave native, disemboweled
made free by loss
eviscerated
lost with the others now
in ameri**K**a.

The money gods have taken over the mass mind
oh, continent of the Un begun, refined
you miserable war mongers
upside down in your own darkness
walking with the beast
in Babylon
blinded by increase
killing off the poor in intervals
tip toeing ever so closely into complete totalitarianism
I will leave my voice here
in ameri**K**a.

June Barefield

Free at Last

Free of Pettiness
Peculiar to the buttoned up, tight butt, responsible type;
Defiant and contemptuous
Hanging low in that tricky aura between dream and death
And trivial things
Like unanswered eyes
And lifeless devices, illuminating the skies
An unrealized nirvana of the mind
Where we hide our truth and disguise our smiles.
And God turns His head when you sit quietly in thought
Where laughter is fought for
And genuine laughter killed
Spilled like oil in oceans.
So, nothing is mine but time.
This provocateur, always in motion
Free of pettiness.

Peculiar to the "believe the evening news," vote or die, keep shit in perspective-type
Revealed openly and succinct
With distinction
Like mother's madness, and memoirs of darkness
Mindful of Christ, the eternal humiliant.
The insane tyrant
Where He, mother, and several other corpses hold me tightly in their arms
And beautifully smothered charms
Where memories die in weather-worn photos, and the wind-frayed sound of a distant city
FREE . . .
Free of pettiness.

Stay Human

Turn

Instead of going up
I turned.
Unlearned, I veered, descending RIGHT
Then LEFT.
Unkempt, inept and unconcerned, insecure and uncertain
Devoid of something, but for my depths, my deceptions
I turned, spending a lifetime convalescing
Frightened by rejection.
A deceitful revelation, ingested
Devoid of something
Descending.
Never particularly tender, at least on the outside.
Inside, I am being eaten alive
Born just about rugged enough to keep up.
I keep turning.
Left then right, ruNnING
"B4 the Dawn"
Before I ascend
Climb the hilL
eYe turn.
Often, I have had to strike to fend off and fight.
I have also resisted
Attacked!
My reaction for an infraction
The only way to resist without paying the exact cost.
Lost . . .
Descending.
These, the demands of a life, lived, apprehended
This life given to me
Dishonorably unmentioned.
The sort of life I have blundered into.
I have seen the devil of violence and greed
Even shook his hand in a pledge of falsehood and conceit
The devil of want and need, I have indeed gleaned
The devil of my hot, unquenchable desire
Conspiring against myself.
This devil am I

June Barefield

Descending.
So, let the stars, the moon, and the Earth Herself bear witness to this.
These are the strong, RED-eyed, passionate, healthy devils of one's wish
Wishing & dreaming on the chain gang, leaning towards a meaning without meaning.
Now, eYe stand on some hillside, appalled
And without forethought, I foresaw
Inside the blinding sunshine of my mind's eYe
Almost as if by warning
Parallel to this truth of yearning
Perpendicular to the pious folk, them claim deserving
Turning.
I avoid an enormous hole some flabby, weak-eyed, devil has for me prepared
Another pitiless folly, felled.
Again
I turn
Ascending slowly now
Learning and growing now.
Let the stars, and the moon, and the Earth Herself bear witness now!
Impossible to divine anyhow
I stroll into the shade for a moment now.
Head up, eyes open now.
A bit weary now
Humbled somehow.
Ascending
eYe turn.

Imagine

From the incubated God particle function
Into a world of thought
From the ever immortal eYe
Out of darkness, illuminated
Ever-expanding, the human imagination
In the beginning . . .
Word connotation
And light
Like a beautifully kind idea, suddenly transformed into life
In the beginning . . .
A fancy sort of thought hallucination
A phantasm of irrational un-reason
Disobligingly imaginative
And inspired
Faithful in defiance
In tune to this passionate wish
A tone, frequently dismissed.
To imagine this gift
Frequencies shift
To revisit this "myth."
The divine body of man, mysteriously hidden from the ages, realized
Into creation.
The great and all-powerful awakening, creating, again, imagination
Free of limitations
A replication of the everything equation.
The divine mind, born out of creation
Creating the pattern perfectly out of the infinite within.
Imagine this gift.

Open Streets

Whatever's not in the open street, to me, is a bold-faced lie
Admittedly, mostly, the streets are as open, as honest, as the good Xhristian and his Statist Mind
From time to time, inside a dreamer's eyes, something else, something pure, something uncontaminated is realized
Observation is underrated
But observation is key.
Listen while you observe
Watch them all proclaim truth that they might testify to a lie
The lie
The people of this lie
This incredibly credible lie
Finessed favorably in sections
Injected directly into your pattern of thought by Corporate Television diatribe
Live tonight on CNN News where they sell you the Blues
And advertise a reality, secretly despised
For the hearts and the minds
All of it contrived.
They, them, those, whose authorities procured through duress while they connive.
Participants complicit, apathetic and listless
AND PARTICIPATION IS THE PEOPLE'S GREATEST DOWNFALL!
This, one mustn't forget:
Everything is for sale
Everybody
Everywhere
ALL THE TIME
Greed is virtuous
Compassion vice
Everything is under a spell
Everything has a price
Everyone, a salesman, attempting to mimic his oppressor.
Build a "brand"
Just another sluggard amongst the others, smothered in comparison with his brother
BRANDED
Competing
Programmed
CONTROLLED.

Stay Human

One Nation
One mold.
Everything's for sale.
Consumption is the third rail; so, consumptions prevail.
Them testify to a maniacal type matrimony, divorced and demeaned dastardly, for the derived derivatives of the over-inquisitive, simply living the lie given to them, and all of it, for dividends.
Ultra-synthetic and frenetic
All ornamental aesthetic
So, **NOT** compelling.
A *reaL nigga* stuck in this void should be issued some sort of repellent
Framed to the everyday doldrums mantra.
Ask a 35yr-old *today* about the BLACK PANTHERS, but don't expect any intelligent, informed answers.
The crippling expectation of this unattainable dream
Merely a comparison narrative
Got 'em killing for fun on every street.
The Mass Mind, slipping into a darkness perceived as light.
Not speaking out is ordinary.
To fight against the dominant tendencies, a repugnant function frowned upon in the human assembly line at every junction.
And what them call the constituent?
Indicating an unrelated, ill persuasive, inter-relation
Like a face, the nation-type fakeness
Lavender ladies, like calendar daily's, birthing Rosemary Babies.
Rinse and repeat, competing always for an almost maybe.
Comfortable with their enslavement
Right-brained and unbalanced
Engineered and emasculated.
Insert inertia and eliminate any challenge not paid for
Enacting the inexact
Only to interact over and again without facts being demonstrated
THIS MESSAGE: Castrated for culture at this picnic-4-vultures
From legislation to human nature
And all that bullshit, debated across the nation on TV stations
2+2=5.
The answer you've accepted calcified, particularly, for the pacified;
Specifically, a cultural bribe.
Now, all of your "good words," mere sentences on disguised death warrants
Served up to savage souls of their freedom.

June Barefield

God given, tethered tenderly in revelry
Thought-processed for ownership, recited so heavenly;
A deliberate attack, deliberated from incubation
All receipts, accumulating.
For, the love of money need not reason but ransoms
Written in canons like anthems
And of course, there remains . . .
The Open Streets
The good Xhristian and his Statist Mind
The bold-faced lie
And **the people**
The people of this lie.

Shadow

Don't know if it's the screaming for you inside my head

Or the silence where I forgot you ever existed.

To revisit the sounds

I've forgotten

To listen

And wait

Waste away, like time

In the shadows.

Screaming

Inside my head.

I just don't know.

June Barefield

Haze

All the stars in my city are running back to the sun
I hardly ever see them anymore
But I'm watching
And there's something wicked in the air
Something wicked does this way come
Feels to me like despair
Are you watching?
Can you feel it?
There's a constant haze over the city, and it's everywhere
Even in the evenings
There's this dreary dilemma, diluting the energies
Blocking the stars
In us
Running back to the sun
Shrinking
In a fog of haze.
Plan your escape you must, from the cities.
I believe that my beautiful Moon Goddess has got to be just beside
Herself by now.
Pesky, ungrateful, dastardly, humanoids!
We're blocking out the sun!!
The stars are on the run,
Purposely.
Personally, my fascination with the stars began at an early age
To stargaze
I survived many a fad, but the stars remain.
I'd lay out on my daddy's garage, amazed!
Those were good days!!
I took them for granted though
The small things
A glorious wonderment only God can explain
And trust me when I say, I've made my inquiries.
But i think that God's reply, the **Earth** herself must explain
It's Nature's Way.
By the way,
Am I the only one looking up into the firmament for guidance and rest today?
Into the constellations, searching for a familiar face?

Stay Human

To embrace the almighty ones as the moments disappear, then reappear as something else?
Somewhere else, yet somehow remain the same, like time and space?
To be replaced by this dirty Grey haze?
The stars
Our stars
They're running away
Back to the sun.
A sort of helplessness that's difficult to explain.
A containment
A discomforting, like
The tightening in my chest, the shortening of my breath.
I can feel it.
Despair, exhaled.
It seems that every exit ramp is being disappeared.
The stars are running back to the sun.

Ideation

Disastrously
Full circle, i have come.
This destination does manifest
A dreadful sense of calm.
Sleep is all I seek.
Self-hatred, my esteem.
Night terror is the dream
Joyless and dank.
It seems, my pain, them call depression.
A fractured expression
Dark infection
An all-time anxiety congestion.
My day-to-day existence, without concession
Dumbed down with the doldrums of a mistake them call living.
Ideation is death, all i think is dying.
All i know is i know absolutely nothing but compliance, even in my defiance.
I've just grown so tired of trying
Tired of lying to myself.
This destination does manifest.
Disastrously
Full circle, I have come.

Stay Human

Facade

I wear a mask when I step out the door
Straight-faced, for protection
Mugg on mean, disconnected
Survival, the technique learned from a society's insane projection
And separate
A spectacle
A portrait painted for the presumption of my existence
The only thing that's consistent is this idea of mine concerning resistance
Innocence long since gone
So, I adopt "the lie" to get along
Sing those imaginary freedom songs
And all of this is my fault
All of it
I'm desperate to survive but I hate living, pretending that this is life
In survival mode
Motivated by the fear of the unknown, but not really though
I procrastinate because I hate this insistence on image
I am lethargic and apathetic because I have too much resentment about living
I am utterly uncommitted
I daydream at night
About things, I would never say
In the daytime, I am 1,000 miles away
I stargaze and meditate, contemplate, and consider mere moments for hours
Deliberate over happiness and despair to examine my personal atonement as I cower
I wish I could just fly away!
I've lost my way before I realized a "way" existed
Before I believed in comparing narratives and ignoring unprincipled competition

The world is sadistic
In me
A facade
Conflicted most days with twisted visions of inhumane sedition
I mock the so-called "citizen"; so, the clock is ticking
Fully realizing, I'm not much different,
Stuck in the muck, trying to duck the same stupid traditions
A generational sickness
I'm swayed by the sameness because the facade never changes

June Barefield

This portrait was painted to be duplicated
I meditate daily on the life of my children
Bogged down by the civilized contriver on every channel
At every stop
Around every corner
Cornered now because I've somehow discovered me in the division
A facade
I moved away for a bit to contemplate underneath an Arizona moon
The skyline, magnificently lit up with stars
But every time I get out, "they" pull me back into this familiar fishbowl, where all the guppies pretend to be sharks
Where the civilized bribe one another and present it as love
Where the charade is fantastic until the moment it's not
Convinced that the evidence is cogent enough
Poignant and potent but completely a bluff
So, I hide my smiles and I stifle my screams
My identity is identical to everyone I know
A facade
Well-mannered manikins with manicures and fully oxidized pinky toes!!
When I walk out the door
Facade protection is like insurance for medicine
I'm just another specimen, getting along for the sake of the oxygen
So, I hold my breath . . .
Swayed by the sameness because the facade never changes.
I exhale every time and reconsider life's quest
It's got to amount to more than this
. . . Facade

Stay Human

Bang!

To lives not always conducive to the word
"Life"
Hypocritical and absurd
"To Live"
Such a puzzling contradiction to live inside of the herd
Existing
Drifting towards complete subsistence
Mind-weakening
Afraid of hell and dying because someone told me I will burn eternally
Internally, I am already on fire
A demon dwells somewhere inside my mind
Like Screw-Tape or Wormwood, facilitating my helplessness in pleasure, as they pick
Then pluck around my semi-conscious nonsense, testing and teasing all of these seemingly pleasing pleasure buttons
They push anger, and then titillate it for a spell, knowing I am fighting for my very sanity
It seems, I always fail
S . . . oooone . . . r or, later the demon of rage and contempt rings the opening bell
I fight my demons well enough, but when I win; they slide in another fate, and open up another gate
A porthole to lust takes hold, and sooner or later, I take the bait
I conquer lust, and now I am gluttonous, lazy, hateful
It's crazy
And so hard to trust
I have this dereliction for virtue
Feels like I am being watched all the time, and I am see-thru
InvisiBle, not worthy, my vanity is unnerving
I am out of sorts
To value my deficiency only makes it worse
I am cursed, cracked, I lack the conviction to follow through
Always, am I, falling short of something I would "like" to do
And lately, I cry a lot for nothing
Something's bluffing whatever is left of the lovely inside of my nugget
Fuck it!
Give me drugs and alcohol, I'd like to quiet the voices echoing down through these wicked halls
Mind mutiny and maliciousness frame the pretense to another episode, complete with ill-intent

June Barefield

Bent on the disruption of my circadian cycles
I am leaning ever so closely to once again picking up the assault rifle
Trifling down the path to utter despair. Beware!
My thousand-yard stare, I compare to the hopelessness in the air
Everywhere
There's a war going on that no one can see but me, or they don't care
I feel too deeply
Think too freely
But I have zero hold on the anxiety in the cold downpour of my hallowed soul
I contemplate . . .
BANG!
& Just get it over with
. . . Hesitant

That would destroy my mother
Smother whatever she has left to covet
She'd be all alone
The inverse order of the stone's
UNKNOWN.
I'm just a cowardly drone
To acquiesce to my assent, relent, and slowly soften to this sickness
My demented possessiveness & hostile unfaithfulness
My corrupted zeal
My desire
Me
Mine
I
I want to die!
I really would like to know the truth about the other side
Nothingness iz an appetite
BANG!
& Just get it over with!!

Horrific horns blow and screech down every corridor
I look frantically for a door
Life is lost, and death unknown in the eyes of the beholder
My last selfish act is to close my folder
BANG!
Pain erased
It's over.

Stay Human

"There will be, in the next generation or so, a pharmacological method of making people love their servitude, and producing dictatorship without tears, so to speak, producing a kind of painless concentration camp for entire societies, so that people will in fact have their liberties taken away from them, but will rather enjoy it, because they will be distracted from any desire to rebel by propaganda or brainwashing, or brainwashing enhanced by pharmacological methods. And this seems to be the final revolution."

Aldous Huxley (1894-1963)

English writer and philosopher

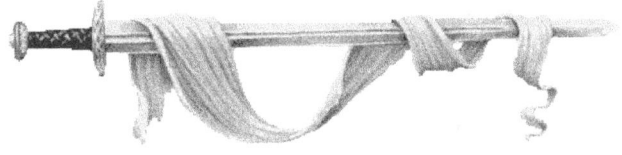

Misremember?

True introspection is a painful process of destruction to unlearn . . . Introspection is the act of self-reflection and rumination. The initial act of self-love is reflection of self. This, the initial act, will require the constancy of your attention's consistency and discipline. If you care enough to "know," then be about that action, painful as it is. The way out is in. Look inside. What them term "cognitive dissonance" is the disease of IGNORE-ANCE, denial & fear. This fear, they use to control you. What you "believe" is at the very precipice of the pathology prescribed for you. Everything you have learned is a lie! To undo the undone is to unlearn.

      The constructs of your cage's design constitute mind-control and the slavery of statism. I encourage you to do the work of introspection, endure the pain and disappointment of becoming self-aware, and ultimately, completely free from all that you "think" to believe. Don't expect to be the bell of the ball! People are not going to be able to see what you see, or feel what you feel. This endeavor to ground yourself in truth and to find real balance and peace is a lonely one, but you are never alone. Get truth, real truth, and unlearn. You must break the patterns of thought, controlling what it is you believe. It is all a lie.

Look inside.

Stay Human

"A thousand times we die in one life. We crumble, break, and tear apart until the layers of illusion are burned away and all that is left, is the truth of who and what we really are."

Teal Swan (b. 1984)

American author

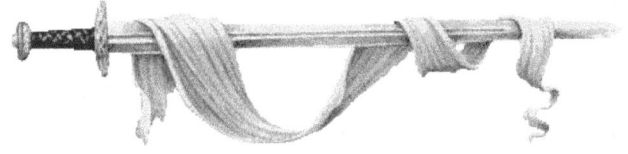

June Barefield

We Die

Amicable and true
Since them people sailed the blue seas with blue eyes and blonde hair in fancy blue suits
Kross in one hand, chains in the other, satchels full of gunpowder
The rape of the world began with the black mother-Earth.
And so we die . . .
We die in AfriKa
Venezuela
Puerto Rico
Brazil
In Peru
We die . . .
Crying over "civil" rights
Begging 2b humanized
In ameriKa
We die over broken tail-lights
Sentenced to death for walking home at night
We die . . .
And we do not fight back

We die . . .
& Then march
We sing
& Then chant
We support a co-opted movement and interview with the enemy
The leadership of said movement, in reality, is the enemy
The "revolution" has now been televised
Instantly wickedness conflates the energy
Cleverly, all momentum is made irrelevant
Allowed to be pepper-sprayed
Engaged with rubber bullets and CS gas until eleven

We die . . .
With smartphones in the garment district
Pledging allegiance to celebrity
He died with a dream about achievement
She died afraid to live, but "believing"
Believing in an afterlife after life
Fairy tales of heaven
Murdered on earth
Cursed them say is Cannan

Stay Human

Obedience to the master
Emphasized so eloquently by the Pastor
Captured by religion, still on the slave ship "Jesus"
Subservient to the overlords
Waiting on the rapture
& So, we die . . .
The after-effects of whatever television has left for you
In a trance called life
Hollering, "hands up, don't shoot!"
To shoot back, shoot first, to unite, temporized by those that control you
Terrorized by those given unholy authority over you
"Fuck the police," right?
Micha Johnson shoots back, and we demonize him too
The ultimate sacrifice given
Rest in power, Mr. Johnson
Mr. Johnson died living
Any consensus at all with you in mind? A mere continuum of genocide
In Palestine
Venezuela
Chile'
Haiti
Jamaica
Lebanon
In THE CONGO
We die . . .

In black skin,
Masked in a white mind, phony and polite,
Waiting for our children to grow up and work
Destination suburbia where even "God" is good
Clean-cut negropean, comfortable enough to comply with a smile
And so, we die . . .
In a protestant collection box
Worm supremacy
Always broke
Always owing
Obedient to this new-age enslavement,
Never knowing the geography of the complexion
Companion to the "ideals" of democracy
Infected, tuned in to the evening's propaganda
And every evening
We die . . .
Dreaming fairy tales of heaven.

Passover

It's been said that the Christ Himself scuffed up His knees
A mandatory journey
3 days inside the awful underneath
Where every shadow dances madly in the fire's light to be freed
Where walls once deemed impenetrable are penetrated
Gliding gracefully through the ghost of change for change's sake with such ease
And free of pain on Savior's day
But no change
Where dreams have nametags, pinned on fat black flies with gluey white eyes
Nursing grievances and whiskey, projecting the lie through a smile beguiled
Apprehensive and enclosed, a silent riot inside, exposed
Where life-sized crucifixes transfix, empty, infantile, reptilian mind-states
Without insight, only hate
Symmetrically postured
Putrid & dank
Imposing some announcement artificially memorialized
Opposing only goodness
Profanity oozing from under every single door
And loathing

But no one is passed over.

Through these corridors
There's a national crisis amongst the damned
A life hereafter is spoken of, but no one believes it, not really
From the bottom up blinded to everything but want & desire
For plundered pockets and dignity
The indignant and his increase
For plastic cards & bank notes
Cut throat in turncoat and starched shirts
Fucking one another
All impersonally conceived, mounted like false teeth, green with the envy that Babylon
The "New Babylon" has achieved in deceit by thieves
Into the nostrils where death breathed the lie of life into an already dead being
MACHINES.
Through these corridors
Mongrels and whores
Vagabonds and rapists

Stay Human

Saints for Satan control this monetary enslavement
Citizens are only patients
Impatiently awaiting
To die
Impotent and vacant
Like a soft dick sliding out of the must and damp trap, tricking the
    docile little vermin again
Waltzing in and out of semi-consciousness with the other rats
Clapping on command
Nibbling at dangling bits and pieces of humiliation, slaver pouring from off of lips
Life-sized crucifixes transfixing, empty, infantile, reptilian mind-states
Unaware
Where The Christ Himself once scuffed up His knees
Or so the story goes
Between heaven and earth, in hell
Impatiently waiting
Through these corridors, **death speaks**
But no one is passed over.

June Barefield

Who Will Do?
*Another Un-poetiK **Rant!***

The minds of men, they've mapped for centuries
Them titillate the tendencies to tamper down the energies
But, who the fuck is "they"?
Them
Those unexposed philanthropic platitude creators
They've existed from the Iron Age to Rome
"Them"
The invaders and takers, the moneybook makers, the enslavers and creators of this perversion of reality
"They"
The marauders and murderous villains, brothers of the black sun, the chameleons
The first unholy ones from the start of human memory
"Them"
Play you like the strateverous in the chorus of your enemies
Create this peasant competition, a hunger game soliloquy
"They"
Keep you fastened to the reality, accepted so willingly
Trained us for obedience devotedly
However:
To connect a dot or two is to discover the treachery that innately you already knew
But "knowing" is not enough, is it?
That part about the 7 angels with the 7 vials, the 7 plagues
Beseeching a great city, shining atop a mighty mountaintop where faithfully "they" control the peasant class
The Mass-mind, in total compliance
"They" own the knowledge
"They" educate your children to grow up and do their bidding
And we bend the knee, bowing down low at the tabernacle of our very own abasement
Enslaved in this training that new-age slaves get
So, get this:
Knowing is not enough.
To just know:
The part about the renewing of one's mind, and the battle of the principalities, and the powers of this world being the rulers, the very darkness of this "world"
Replicated in you and me
Recreated to be duplicated to fit nicely into the times
The imitation of the human-kind
From the age of stone and iron up until the desecration of AI
"Them"

Stay Human

They use fear to control you
A delusional state of comparisons and false narratives
The clarity them seek is control of the chaos
A Hegelian narrative, and no-thing, including human beings, is sacred
Humanity, butt-naked, bathing in the hatred, forsaken
Just ask any brave native to explain the murderous raping, taking the souls of men
Pulling the levers, leveling everything
We keep forgetting to remember the essence in the aether, magically turned into confetti
They are building back better now
Considering:
The script that flips and flops from snoot to ass, as the wealthy pose and smile on your Television; but in private, they just laugh
So, who's the ass?
Not "they."
It's fear controlling this gigantic stock of human cattle:
Us.
We are that ass!
In fact:
The fear is fanned by your friendly neighborhood propaganda swillers
The fluoride-addled zombies, us, comply
We don't even know why
Or ask why
Or think to try and realize a new, more self-reliant lie
Why?
"They,"
Your government is both dope dealers and killers, but mostly just actors
And so, a Democrat told a Republican that their masters fund both sides
Consider:
In Palestine, we starve; in ameriKa, we lie
The synagogue of Satan is an Ashkenazi operation of the khazarian empire
Tribe of Japheth, pretending to be Semitic, controlling the Mass-mind . . . forever?
But just knowing is not enough
Is it?
I'm beginning to understand why my brother kept his eYe on the 13
Everything being everything, reality being no-thing
I'm thinking that maybe that's why all the stars over the cities are running back to the Sun
To rediscover something meaningful is to undo the undone
But what is done?
And who will do?
Not them.
Us.
We must do.

"Until they become conscious, they will never rebel, and until after they have rebelled, they cannot become conscious."

Eric Author Blair, Pen Name: George Orwell (1903-1950)

British novelist, poet, essayist, journalist, and critic

Stay Human

This Night

Rebel: I give you the night,
This night,
And over time, this night shall accost you, invoke you, only to finally beseech, and then salute you
You must struggle and learn
This beckoning, vibrating within you, guides you
Becoming this reckoning requires not violence
Silence is everywhere inside of you now
It frightens you,
This silence
It's taken the suffering and violence of the ancestors' ages to create this quiet within you, my little rebel
Inside where your breath rests, and fields and flowers, and glow worms and stars hang on to every word spoken
UNBROKEN
A vivid, rich, brilliant, remembrance
. . . Of Me
Embrace this singed hush and sudden metamorphosis
Let it hail down in a fatal triangular calm
Three points, ONE circle
This, the only reality, requires complete concentration and focus
This Night.
Underneath a great black hole, where perhaps I should have buried you many moons ago.

Rebel: Embrace this singed hush,
This sudden metamorphosis,
It is **eYe**,
Contend no longer with the unequal sun
Dance!
Dance that broken yoke dance amongst my calabash of pregnant stars
. . . eYe give you the night
RISE NOW.

June Barefield

bird
(Thank you, Jack.)

i jumped today and i survived
everyone assumed that i wanted to die
thought secretary, perhaps
hoping, maybe, i would die
UNAWARE, i jumped anyhow
now i see
but not only with my eyes
motivated always by unreasonable reasons
i jumped today
jumped for freedom
there's a time to die
but it ain't my time
i just wanted to know what it's like to fly
I'LL JUMP AGAIN TOMORROW
come, let us jump together

Stay Human

Swan

Tell me your story,
Where'd you first appear?
What dark sands are you reaching for?
Where do you rest b4 the dawn arrives?
What are you searching for,
Swan?

I think.
In doing so, I know you've found a place of majesty and grace
A place where spirit is in bloom, and depression does not exist
A place where freedom is free, and life, real
Oh, how I long to see what you see
Suspend for me all of my disbelief,
My beautiful swan.

I have smelled the aroma of the great I am, for a second, at least, maybe two
I've been captured inside the magnificence of servitude
I conclude that you have too, my beautiful Swan
Spirit determines what is
I must choose.
Swan, I choose you.
Please, tell me your story.

June Barefield

Question Mark Missing

What is it
& Where did it go?
Whatever "it" is, I lost along with my ignorance
At least, most of it
I think, maybe, it's possible that I know
. . . That I know absolutely nothing at all. I'm just watching the show!
Wondering, who stole the harmony?
Where did it go?
And what is this impenetrable silence, searching for that ineffable "self", ripping and twisting, rooting out all the demons of this flesh
Must I forever digress
Please, tell me why contentment is really only contagion
Just another ungodly arrangement, to be content with a change that never changes from the hands of the money changers
While the mon-eYe is fake?
And what the fuck is **God**
    but enslavement and shame
Simply an engagement, arranged by the enslavers that shackled me to this dream
This freedom dream
My destiny manifests process
Processed for ownership
While the horsewhip and pistol grip-repress any and all protest on the citizen-ship
But them folk tell me that, when I am strong, I am weak
"Fuck them people," keeps it all in its proper context for me
I spread my canvas to the breeze
"Them people,"
They keep the diaspora of me on their knees
Begging and pleading, and eager to please
Praying politely to the alabaster abstraction of their enemies
Tell me why they lie?
Why I am condemned with this conditioning to "believe"
In a trance called life
In this constant search for "love"
Just numb and overcome
Wondering, beseeching, seeking, searching, questioning the questions that the answers don't fulfill?
What is it?

Stay Human

Where did "it" go?
Who stole the harmony?
Will I ever know?
I'm just numb, admittedly overcome
And I keep wondering . . .
What in the fuck am I supposed to do with these bloody gloves?

June Barefield

Progress

Too many bad guys and ghosts
And scary monsters . . .

The dreadful spectacle of power is what attracts them all
Consecrated with contemptible sameness
But all sorts of words MAKE flesh.
Follow me now . . .
Draw back the curtain on the depravity of man
Thwart this idea of progress.
A false idea
Progress.
The horizon's never been more vertical
The Tower at Babel, resurrected
In God, the will to nothingness is sanctified
A structure concept, system, practice
Cold malice
Decadence, ascending in the name of increase, with a particular artistry for religion.
Draw back the curtain.

Too many bad guys and ghosts
And scary monsters . . .

Stay Human

Asylum

In a world system
To survive, one must master the art of perjury
To save your castle, you must sacrifice a bishop, whose primary function is to eliminate the pawns
You know, keep all the niggas off the lawn
Keep 'em maintained at an arraignment
In a Kourt House venue; so, the Castle and the Knights may institute the King's law
Where the deception of authority paints truth with disgustingly, ugly brushes
Constructs of the asylum before destruction
The judges, fuck 'em!
They are just puppets.
Honor, also merely an act of defense
Fiendish oaths sworn over a Holy Book.
All pretense
An antagonizing of the protagonists
But **kneegros** stay on trial.
So, Order in the Kourt!
Where the lie and the truth must "feel" the same
It's in the language
And after confirmation of this skill
Truth has no validity.
Truth means nothing at all
But I am told that love remains
And love is pain

In the asylum
People prefer to just be entertained.
The picture, painted perfectly by those appointed to pontificate.
So, every innocence is properly executed to be tethered heavenly
While every crime of the ruling class has been excused.
After all, they've created the "rules."
So, abuse of power becomes the people's muse.
Confused?
Follow me now . . .

The people "believe"
Listening intently to the Hunger Game managers propagandize the National News
I observe.

June Barefield

The people "follow"
From ignorance to influence into the inference of insolence.
Collectivism, the schism, group thought like real religion,
. . . But what is real?
The computation of mass consumption
And for the people, "watching" the obsolescence of humankind
Them selling mirrors in cities occupied by the blind!
An altered sort of state where the lumpen proletariat are merely steak for the rich.
And the truth?
Truth means nothing at all
Although, them say, love remains
But love is pain.

In the asylum
Love is transactional;
Grace, genocidal
And all is fate.
Confused?
In a world system
2+2=5.
Just take a look outside!
All are assembled so cleverly to resemble the other inmates in the asylum.
ATTENTION, WAL-MART SHOPPERS!
Embryo after embryo, pushed through the same corrupted womb to be entombed, alive
Born to work, pay taxes, and then die
. . . This is life
In tune with a dastardly spell
Controlled with words like "freedom" and "justice" and "democracy" and "God"
But everybody's 4sale
Infected with the virus of a conformity existence
Kneeling together at the altar of statist abasement.
In a world system.
Enslavement, a coordinated predetermination
A diabolical, devilish corporate arrangement
And marching, dressed to the right in columns of four.
It's Johnny!
Johnny has come marching home from war
But the lie and the truth, they don't "feel" the same anymore.
A pawn of elitism is he
Torn

Stay Human

Duality, twisted into knots
Heart, filled up with larceny
His visions are sadistic.
He knows now betrayal.
So now, his reality is different
In tune to a spell he can never break completely.
His entire actuality is missing
Constantly reminded of his fellow pawns.
Night terrors and apparitions.
Who is he?
His family can't recognize him anymore
Simply an inmate at the asylum where them annihilate the poor.
Johnny keeps his hands in his pockets now, stumbling around the VA Hospital, re-upping
On his psychotropic
STUCK,
And the world wants him stuck.
The world, it does NOT give a fuck.
But, "thank you for your service," nigga!
His retrogress is addressed politely enough, over and again
In the asylum
From oxycodone to gabapentin to whatever drug them use to pacify the best of men.
Johnny made it home, but Johnnie's a mess.
He must begin again
Fiendishly, conveyer-belted into hell
On Earth
In a world system
At the asylum.
And still, I'm told, there is love,
And I believe that there is.
There must be!
Love . . .
But love,
Love is pain.

Destiny

It has its way of ranging us all shoulder to shoulder, trampling whatever remains of our solitude
The splinter in wound shall proclaim only unity; in suffering
A strengthening of aptitude
Only then
Out of desperation
Together, our destiny does manifest
Ranging us shoulder to shoulder, growing older without a stone for the sling, only this slow, biter sting, called life
And so it goes, mixing together the mortar of brotherhood, where destiny must call out over the dust of idolatry
When every impulse must be freedom
And only out of desperation
Our destiny does manifest
A restoration
A reconstructing
Out of desperation
Shoulder to shoulder
TOGETHER,
Our destiny does manifest.

Stay Human

ameriKan me

I keep trying to figure out just exactly what it means to be an American
It makes me angry, too
I look inside myself unashamed though
I try to make sense of my family in America
I can see slavery and sharecropping, some Kiowa woman, native to this land, and
I see Germany
Never really got off into astrology
But I can see Mars
The land of the free
America?
I just don't see.
So, with no recognition of what it is that makes me American,
I think about what it really means, what it takes to be a true
American.
I see black women trying so hard to be American.
I see black men with three piece minds, trying hard to be American.
I think back to all the times I stood up out of my seat and pledged allegiance
      to this thing, America.
And still, so many years later, I cannot hear my own footsteps inside the lyrics of
This thing . . . America.
I can see the struggle every single day
And I feel the pain.
I humble myself at times, and try to embrace this strange place, America.
The RED and the White
The Blue, too.
I see them talking on TV.
We're made to feel paramount, yet, the African inside this America
He is obsolete.
I've defined freedom.
America ain't it.
Freedom?
Freedom's a waterfall in America, falling down all around me
It all falls down in America.
   . . . ameriKan me.

June Barefield

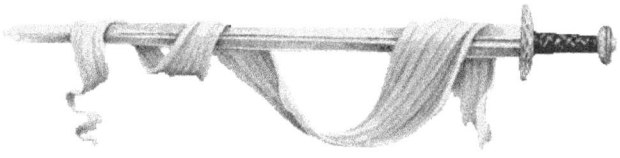

"Jails and prisons are designed to break human beings, to convert the population into specimens in a zoo — obedient to our keepers, but dangerous to each other."

Angela Davis (b. 1944)

American Marxist and feminist political activist, philosopher, academic, and author

Stay Human

Thought Babel
A Head-Gut Invocation

Paradise of mind
Nirvana
To live life alive
To thrive unreasonably in the knowledge that
The reasonable cannot love find
Not ever.
But reasonable is **relative** to one's condition.
Ask any constituent.
A popular insight comparative
A marketable sedation repairative.
Relatively speaking, the narrative
The competitive manner in which one is trained to deal with
"The world"
A dreadful plight
Where the dumb sell mirrors to the blind.
So, my boots stay laced up tight
Knowing I might gotta freeze
Some nights.
Always, since the beginning of time
The reasonable cannot love find.
Not in this life
Or the next.
Next time I come back
I wanna fly, see if I can find my mother
And apologize.
My premonitions of preparedness . . .
To shake all the baggage of my inheritance.
And the same generational darkness that sparked this Mind's State
One day will be a raging fire
Militant because my mind is mine
I think my own thoughts.
Reality, a smack in the face from the paw of a lion.
Personally, I've been smacked a thousand times!
And everybody, lying
All the time
While they wait in line
Thinking about a lie.

June Barefield

The proper, most **reasonable**, lie,
Tuned in unknowingly to the wicked melody of the times.
A tri*tone in* the fourth and seventh degrees, like F and B played on the major scale of C
In the diabolical, one dimensional, semi-tone of 6ix
Out of focus, but fixed
Taking pictures
Faking smiles
Bringing well-trained monsters to life
And the worst of the zombie-class
Plastic crocodiles
Pretending to be kind
The always-compliant type.
But still
The power of love lies between one's heart and one's nuts.
So, check nuts!!
I'm surmising that negros just ain't suffered enough.
But I don't know
Perhaps they just don't give a fuck.
With every weight and all the pain that this life provides
Only one word alone will suffice:
Love.
But the work is pain
As it should be.
So, watch their actions after they say whatever they say.
They say so much
All the time.
The test of faith is to endure
And learn
But to think upon these things
Whatever is pure and patient
Whatever is good
Whatever is lovely and sure
To make "care" the number one concern
To care.
The suggestion, questioning the testing for what them Jesuit negros call a blessing
A redressing, attesting to a destination
A migration of sorts
Of mind
A head-gut invocation
Thought Babel,

Stay Human

Tracing the tracks of the teary eye
Until the reality of life does inspire
Motivation does arise
Back to enter again into the center
To begin life's adventure
Adventure after adventure
A treasure wrapped up tightly inside a sackcloth
An enigma
Lost, but not forever.
Duplicity, one must dominate with the simplest plan
Remember?
Free of the magical box where we cut ourselves in twos
And only after we've scorched every earth in attempt to find worth
Looking always outside ourselves
"Believing," not being ourselves
Fooling ourselves to find a voice.
Still, the choice is yours
And one must choose.
So, head up, eyes open.
The reasonable cannot love find, this paradise of mind.
This is real life.
One must choose.
Remember?
Choose love.

June Barefield

Unreasonable, Always

Slammers and Barbarians
The Unbearables, OUTLAWS, and Samerians
Outright contrarians, one and all
Them dance that broken yoke dance, then laugh
Those that wear it all, but have no sleeves
The very last to believe in anything, but Life & Love
Definite, concerning the difference between want
& NEED
Unreasonable, always.

For the wise and the precious ones
The loyal and the grateful ones
For the faithful
The tenacious ones, giving praise with every step
Ten toes down, vanquishing the bane berry daily for a lifetime until nothing's left
Wary of all the sycophantic, systemizing strategies for the make-believe
The overly comfortable, uncaring wanna be's . . .
Fuck 'em.
Fight 'em.
Fuck 'em once more.
Now FLEE!
BANG& GET IT OVER WITH !
A sort of peace.
No compromise.
No plea
& *Absolutely no reprieves*.
Unreasonable, always.

No fear of death, only respect
Problem-solvable when impossible becomes probable.
Insoluble, huh?
Questioning always the question, because mostly, it's the questions that matter.
Discarding the answers
Climbing the ladder
The ones that live in the rain, and dance
To survive the hurricane when it struck, and get back up
To begin again
Over and again

Stay Human

Again and again
& Again
For the Caucasian and the Mexican
Ameri**K**an and the Afri**K**an
the Asian and the Indian
MAN.
Unreasonable, always.

Conceptual-isms for the marks who ignore truth so them fit in.
Peel back the skin and reveal some heart.
Fire starts from straw until flames are so angry it begins to lick off the dross
Testing Gold
Where the contrarian is ripped down from his Kros**S**, only to rÎse up again and walk
The greatest story ever sold.
Roll back the stone to where authenticity resides
Where balance becomes "belief"
Karma is like synchronicity set on fire
Electricity
This revolution in the streets.

Forget Not

Laws
Made by lawless men
Never forget the innocent
Men
Beautiful, brave, Black
Brothers and Sisters
Rotting
Just wasting away in the Pen
Send a new message out to the Grassroots
Tell 'em, say, "Stand up before death!"
Let there be reason for all the times, in every season
Fear not, be of good courage, and be not dismayed
Give your sons and your daughters something real
To believe in
Never forget that Black
Remains a threat,
And if not, then why have so many premeditated precautions
Been taken in the name of Justice
While all the murders and the malice confront just us?
All the magnified, official lies, covering up the truth,
Stirred in a pot no longer melting but still on fire, blowing up while it burns
Where triangulated fires hit new targets with old objectives upon seemingly new relations
Right here. Right now!
In this, which is our unholy Nation up under Satan
Forget Not
The four baby girls in Alabama
Or The Chicago 6
Never forget Huey and Assata
Or every single nigga in AmeriKa that has ever been lynched
Do not forget Cointellpro and Geronimo Pratt
The eradication of Black Nationalism
And Julio, the rat
Remember all of the dope-infested ghettos
The disparaging hookers in stilettos.
The destruction and annihilation of Black Power
J. Edgar Hoover with his menacing legion of official cowards
Forget Not

Stay Human

While you're out here, still tipping your cap at Obama, giving praise to his momma
Never forget his father
Or any of "the nameless ones who came before but are no more"
"To those who leapt to their salty deaths
To those who battled when all was lost
To those of us who will give birth to gods"
Never Forget
All the unknown burdens, carried in campaign upon campaign, where truth was irrelevant
      yet reverently, they'd remain
Forget Not
Those shot and imprisoned on unsubstantiated charges with immaterial facts, fabricated By
Turn Coats, standing at the Traitors Gate, still claiming to be Black
Now ask yourself, what exactly is The Patriot's Act?
Ask yourselves about all of the mysteries hidden, concerning the revelations of your past
Ethiopia, Egypt
The First Cataract?
Marcus
Medgar
Martin
Angela
Geronimo Pratt?
And forget not to be appalled
This country, Ameri**K**a
Was built on racism and hate, so . . .
Dress every thought with faith, and love, and hope, and Truth
Then sharpen up your razors, iron out your blades, ball up your bullets,
      and when you Must, THEN SHOOT!
Do not hesitate
Just don't ever forget.

What Them Say

That

A coalescence mingled together in combination with this fusion

An amalgamation escalation, shaping the traces of contemplation

Blending hatred and confusion

This and that forsaken

Generations, defaced to erase I am creation

And "time's a wastin"

That's what them say

I do not "believe" them.

Stay Human

Never Tell

With so much to tell,
I'm having thoughts of running away again,
Only to begin again
A terrifying tale, but I'll never tell.
I watch sometimes the people rushing by me, hoping to find some agreement in their eyes,
And I wonder,
Supposing I were to intercept one of my fellow human beings
Just supposing, all of a sudden, out of nowhere, I were to plainly ask a stranger,
"Why do you go on living like you do?"
A simple question, really . . .
I'd probably be arrested!
And why am I not surprised?
I wonder if any of my fellow human beings talk to themselves like I do.
I wonder, really, if there isn't something very wrong with me.
Lots of wondering, but I'm thru wandering.
At least, I'd like to think so
But even if I had another run away, begin again, in me; which I absolutely do not, I'd Never ever tell.
NOPE.
Furthermore, I have absolutely no desire to be a "useful" member of this society.
Society is sick.
Fuck society!
Insanity is the length of the bandwidth humanity is in,
And I have no desire to work or do anything I don't believe in.
Corporations are plantations.
The word "freedom" is just an incantation.
The entire nation is under a freedom spell,
Inoculated and comfortable
But I'll never tell.
NOPE.
Contrarily, my fellow human beings, of whom I know all too well . . .
Well, best I just zip up my lip before I start some shit
But who would'a thunk it, a nigga lived to tell?
Don't trip tho'! I won't tell. Never
NOPE.
Still, I search for agreement in the eyes of others
On main street, down here with me.
I'm wondering what it is exactly the masses think

June Barefield

And why.
If only we'd all just turn off the TV, go outside and discuss what life is supposed to
Really be.
Staring at a house across the street with the manicured lawn,
The attached garage,
The chimney and the basement, complete with furnace for the heat,
All of it is ugly to me.
Every house, lined up one after the other, cut out like cookies from the cutter,
Everybody secretly competing with one another, and so proud of their lawns!
The ridiculous sameness,
An utter absurdity
. . . But
I don't consider the world's condition as I once did.
The world is so much bigger than where I live
Or who I am.
Over half of the entire world, **my fellow human beings,** they live on less than five
    dollars a day,
A gift to the world, I surmise, gifted with eloquence by Christian men.
Oh dear, the wages of these sins, out of which the cesspool of the spirit of work waves its
    magic wand, making slaves out of men,
All the men, like me, built out of the "main street" ingredients in the land of *The Free*,
Makes me want to just run away and begin again, but nobody's after me,
Not anymore.
Only my thoughts chase me now
But I'll never tell.
NOPE.
If I could find the words to convey the message,
Even just to understand the questions,
Them mask the truth so the answers, mostly, are irrelevant.
I conclude that maybe I should rid myself of the false notions I have
    concerning humanity
"Being human" . . .
Maybe this is it?
Still, I think about the contrast,
The contradiction,
Searching for significance,
Wondering . . .
Meanwhile, some child of The Rockefeller Line is sitting on the toilet, placidly wiping his
    ass
But perhaps, he has servants for that!
In the inner city, a gang of hopeless youth, my people, rob a ready teller in ski masks.

Stay Human

The distinction's in the thinking.
I contemplate the contrast
From alpha to epsilon,
Including all of the semi-moronic pawns,
The policemen, soldiers, and all the starkey bureaucrats that hold the bag.
When I look into their eyes, I do not see agreement.
What I see, I cannot describe.
I sense disharmony,
Imbalance.
I just watch and listen.
I see duplicates duplicating.
The only memory held is also the one to forget.
Lots of folk are apprehensive about even making an eye contact,
And why are my Spidey Senses tingling all the damn time?
I think it's fear I see in the eyes of my fellow human beings,
Or maybe I'm afraid
But I'll never tell.
NOPE.
Who the fuck would listen!
What I need is a good fuck from a proper ho, really tho'!
You know, clean out me ball bearings, tame these feelings inside me, if only for a moment,
    pay the bitch, and watch her go
At least I know, there's some agreement in her eyes.
Bless her souL.

June Barefield

A Propositional Plea

Treat the untouchables,
The so-called "elite," and all who do their bidding;
Treat them all the same way you have been treated;
Greet them not;
Disengage;
Separate;
Do NOT "believe";
Never touch what they touch or pray what they pray
This is "Hunger Games," and it's you, citizen, you are the prey.
So, don't repeat what they say,
And if you dare, turn your television off.
Do it today!
It's making their thinking your thinking, that's hypnotizing and shrinking everything.
ORIGINAL, inside of your being,
THINK!
Treat "them" as you have been treated,
Like the plague.
B vague when U see them.
Seek amongst you the humble,
The downtrodden,
The WILLING,
The HUMAN!
B POETRY, like motion.
Iron out your words until they R flat, smooth, and sharpened up like a good knife for when hunting season begins.
Are you ready?
If so, when you speak, may your words feed 5,000;
But if your words cannot be balled up into bullets, or sewn into coats 4 our children and elderly, made into bandoliers for magazines and grenades,
Stay where you are.
You, my friend, have more to suffer, me thinks,
Thinking thoughts of disengagement from the machine.
Follow me now . . .

Your comfort confounds you with grand ideas of participation and democracy.
I propose simplicity,
A minimalist dichotomy.

Stay Human

All you need is less.
Call it a city nigga's philosophy.
Do NOT write 'em or read 'em or accept what they feed ya' while they collectively bleed ya'
I mean, don't love 'em or hug 'em, try to B tricky and dub 'em.
FUCK THEM!
A propositional plea brought to you live and direct from the pieces of me at peace with Me.
THINK!
Think Louder Now.
Simplify your life ameri**K**a
Kill the consumer you've been cleverly groomed to be.
Your pathology is as make-believe as your freedom dream,
A night terror!
You must NOT "believe."
Ever!
Leave this cultural con game ideologue in the bookstores, on bookshelves, collecting up dust for the flies and the leftover, musty, odor of what was for once.
Times haven't changed all that much,
Mass consumption still ain't enough,
And change will never change until the chains R unshackled from the circumference of brain waves, bluffed with this peace idea.
Au contraire,
Ya think?
Think Louder Now.
When you've grown tired of another with the power to anthologize your souls,
When all your goofy options unfold,
When all the talk grows old,
When it is you that is now hungry and cold,
REMEMBER WHAT WE HAVE PROPOSED:
Fuck the "elite"! It's time we get free!
THINK.
Think Louder Now.
A propositional plea . . .

Smile

No longer do I smile at people I'd prefer biting.
Fuck it! I'm free
Reciting "I have a dream" in my nightmares.
A sensibility, distilled from mass culture
This terrible vulture, gorging herself on herself
An evil seed, equipped with a cadre of vice
Stringing together credible images so dumbed down people "believe"
Thinking, "Long live dead Kapitalism!"
But not me
With more than just a touch of contempt
I'll reign over every night like that evil empire terrorist in Palestine
Only to touch the genuine leaf, blowing in the morning light on a gentle breeze
Where every breath is life
And each step must be precise.
So, I watch as the days slide into night once more.
I'll watch the Four Riders emerge from the east until their horses foam into glue.
With more than just a touch of contempt
My knee's torn from supplication while You strengthen me
And again
I don't think I deserve Your mercy
& Still
I'll not smile at the oblivious.
I'll not watch or consume or follow or "believe."

FUCK IT! I'M FREE!

Contrast Defined

aristocratic
civilized
dignified
elegant
gallant
gracious
polite
stately
adulatory
august
ceremonious
chivalrous
civil
complimentary
conventional
cultured
decorous
flattering
formal
imposing
lofty
obliging
polished
prim
refined
studied
urbane
HIGH-BRED
elite

unrefined
impolite
rude
undignified
unmannerly
vulgar
unsophisticated

June Barefield

indecorous
provincial
inelegant
rough
uncivil
unpolished
uncouth
unsavory
boorish
wonted
stock
rife
LOW-BRED
COMMONER

Note the opposite nature and purpose.
The striking exhibition of otherness, of unlikeness.
Consider the pathology of the über-elite.
NOW, EAT THE RICH.

Stay Human

"And I saw three unclean spirits like frogs come out of the mouth of the dragon, and out of the mouth of the beast, and out of the mouth of the false prophet."

Revelation 16:13 KJV

June Barefield

For the Unwashed Masses

Approaching the tipping point,
    The great reveal,
        Death by 1000 cuts . . .
The 990th was not enough
Too many deliriously orchestrated alabaster lambastes
    Problem
        Reaction
            Solution
A predetermined conclusion
    Created confusion
Nudged nimbly, simply that humanity accept its fate
Wait . . .

The end of comfort or contentment
    System failure
        Distribution shut down

Toilet paper race!!
ATTENTION WAL MART SHOPPERS!
At each other's throats about a Double Whopper
    Unconcerned with the enemy
        Standing at the traitor's gate
Follow me now . . .

For all the professional consumers,
Costumed in your beliefs, passively watching all of the thieves,
Trapped, tethered to a SMART device,
Tryna decide which filter is nice,
Shedding the skin of time,
Shredding the care of humankind,
Swallowed up with their vaguely contrived assurances, blind.

But hey, who the fuck is "they"?
Them,
Those who have arranged your organized delusion meticulously,
One faze after another,
From Pearl Harbor, The Bay of Tonkin, 9-11, and into the Covid scam. ALAKAZAM!
Like magic,

Stay Human

A brand new Ameri**K**an Century, live on Instagram.

1,000 points of phony light,
Swallowing up their messages of fear,
Feeding the confusion,
Seared into the part of your mind, now unaware . . .
All of it illusion.
Them.
They beat words into ploughshares so that everything iz unclear,
And to unlearn is unreal
But still . . .
That tummy-tuck hologram, collagen-injected soul reveals a glitch here,
Dashing towards the wastelands in a state of dread and dissatisfaction
Where relief requires an antidepressant and charity legal paperwork, class action,
In reality, the conspiracy is on the evening news . . .
Globalism, "Free trade," Entertainment,
Mental mind-muscle enslavement.
Yet somehow, the horizon's never been more vertical; only the sun has lost its glare.
The Tower at Babel, resurrected.
Beware.
Chemtrails, everywhere.
Twilight is advancing slow,
Accompanied by death.
All thought, being processed for ownership,
A deliberate attack, calculated from incubation in loneliness.
All receipts, accumulating.
Everything, an obfuscation . . .
This vexed nightmare inside a broken cradle that still rocks.

But first 1,000 cuts
    The great reveal
        The tipping point
           Problem
              Reaction
                  Solution

FATE.

Attention, WalMart shoppers!

. . . Wait.

June Barefield

Hourglass

The story is the story of the egoistic mind, drawing you to emote inherited human pain,
Mixed together with the toxicity of a vainly glorious assumption
Assuming
Each reaction is masked in abstraction
Assuming
Distracted from the reality of nature
Without cause, only effect
Reacting
Playing make-believe
Hence: The creation of the counterfeit human being
Engineered cleverly
A vile maxim, conducting this monstrous symphony;
The hidden hand
Maximizing the populous' deranged enchantment
To be controlled
And commanded
Thinking, it's comfort
As the sand sifts through the hourglass
In the valley of the dried-up bones
Prophetic scrolls begin to unfold.

Say to these bones: "I will make breath enter you, and you will come to life."

Stay Human

"If you think you are free, there is no escape possible."

Ram Dass (1931-2019)

American spiritual leader and guru

June Barefield

Negro Telepathy
A Thought Bubble

White man with small child exits elevator on 2nd floor.
Remaining white woman clutches her purse. I laugh to myself devilishly, thinking, "I don't want anything from you, goofy woman! I bet you she's a good Christian† woman too! A Democrat no doubt! I'll bet she's down with black lives matter!"
More laughter, painful laughter ensues . . .
Why is she so afraid? She might turn that television she's watching off for a day or two, tho!
Her ass cheeks, hella' tight tho'.
Poor baby.
Guess I can't blame her. I'm the nigga they won't show her on TV.
Fuck that bitch, tho'!
. . .Ya know?
6th floor. Elevator door opens. White woman finally looks me in the face, fake smile, and then scrambles out quickly.
I laugh out loud!
Door closes.
All alone again.

Stay Human

FLASHbacK

My bedroom used to B so dark I thought I'd become an astronaut.
There was a ferocious crocodile behind my closet door.
I'd lock him inside & hide.
Afraid of the shifting shadows on the wall, the hollering in the hall,
I felt so small, because I was.
Time and again, I would crawl into myself and imagine I was somewhere else.
Never screamed out once, but I wanted help.
I found my comfort outdoors, running & jumping, playing in the streets.
At home, my mother preached,
Ducking left hooks and throwing books, in a corrupted flux of "fuck yous!" & "I don't give a fuck!"
Waiting 4 someone to come in here, and maybe, kiss me goodnight,
Knowing damn well, first they had to finish up their fight.
Heart beating, like the meanest kid on the playground now, though,
But I wasn't.
I'd like to maybe sniff the glue that binds families together,
Maybe get some attention before I reach detention,
B the smart kid just once, and then, just revel in my cleverness.
Never did I sit on my daddy's lap.
Most of the words he had for me tasted a lot like uncooked carp.
To me, he was always a fishy negro.
It would take a little time, but soon enough, I'd imitate the fool and steal all his fuckin' liquor.
Every now and then, my momma would swing me in her arms like a chandelier,
And that was nice, but fleeting.
Mostly though, to be precise, for as long as I can remember,
All I ever wanted to do was just **breaK** something.

Panic

It sets in quickly

Too quickly

Without any sort of fault line;

Always at work

And working overtime.

A consternation crime

Like an ill-fated muse of mine

Devastated by desire

On fire.

I need a fault line.

Stay Human

Omitting eYe

I omit eYe
The first person
ME
And there's noBody eYe know as well as I.
So, out of a begrudgingly, almost belligerent respect for egoism
Unaware
AT THE CENTER OF "SELF"
The exaltation of self
Unconscious,
Feeding this energy
The imaging of images
This imagery, branding me, conforming me into what's been accepted as
NORMALCY
Shaping and molding the lie--- Omitting eYe.
A collective cancellation in the narrowness of experience to experience this
For I
Confirming my resignation out of the desperation of "ME"
I omit eYe
Expressing an impartial, mostly inept outsider's observance of this humane state
Inside
A proliferation of the profane
For vanity's sake
Committed to uncertainty
For false pride
Commuted to emergency
UN-urgently
Lethargic
Slothfully envious of what he got
Or why she's not
U.
Omitting eYe!
Committing genocide
Claiming a faith
An unholy lie
Considering for moments not what is respectable
But what is falsely respected, and now credible, digestible, and edible.
This is where I shrink from the cold, dreary misery of me.
OMITTING **eYe**
Unaware
The first person . . . Me.

Half

Half-angry manifesto, half-neighborhood love letter . . .

For Kathy and Karla and Tracy and Terry,
Could of done better
For Adel and Rosylin and
Michelle and Nicole.
For Monica,
Should have done better.
She deserved so much better.
A validation of my ego, my impulses.
Too many people suffered for me to grow,
Just to maintain my own and come to a place where I think, I might, maybe, **"know."**
City shit,
Impractical, predictable, impersonal, dispassionate city shit.
My manifesto,
Written in pain
And confusion,
Anger,
Insecurities and delusion,
A creative struggle endeavor.
A letter,
About love
& Survival,
A creation story,
SouL inventory,
And just in the nick of time,
B4 reprobate mind,
Suddenly, eYe blinded by light.
No glory on my personal road 2 Damascus,
Only pain.
Insight,
A long walk thru a dark night until dawn
From pawn to Rook to Bishop to Knight,
Back to pawn,
And my contempt for the King, spawned from my very conception.
This lesson, one must refine thru each testing,
A cleansing clarified to concentrate on the blessing,
An ongoing understanding of this world's deception,

Stay Human

In me, defined;
Not to mention, the joy, the pain, the sacrifice into the suffrage of a forever-connection.

For the essence of meaning, for moments,
A momentum, realized
To create a better ledger,
Hidden, like a city nigga's sand script,
Defiance, written in the hieroglyphics of my soul.
Each experience
In every void,
A transference of revealing
And souL work,
The destruction of image upon the path to self-Mastery,
Overwhelmingly, capturing me,
A constant reminder of life,
Of ideas
And experience;
Un-thinking, if you will, all of the thoughts manufactured for me
By the machine,
Separation from The Hive Mind collective
My manifesto,
The un-learning, a rejection reflected in a dream, written out angrily in desperation to be
Free,
To feel something real,
Something other than fear
Of death
And life.
I saw it in my mother's eyes the day before she died,
The fair Lady Elizabeth . . .
When every one of my Angels cried,
And although it took some time,
Time I did not deserve,
Time
To disengage from the control center of my ego.
Underneath it all,
Where I talk to God
Watch for God
Wait for God
And listen,
Aware of the duplicitous contradiction in life,
The unbeatable "why,"

June Barefield

A world within a world,
A journey manifest to know one's own mind within these worlds inside,
Toiled and dried, plodded and pushed by the inevitability of time, the truest killer,
Searching for Earth
Into and out of the heart of everything for nothing.
To enter into betrayal of self, avoid the curse,
The first major truth on the path of the capable,
A bitter pill indeed,
A pill better men than me could never swallow.
Yet, somehow I did.
To be made empty and hollow,
And deserve it,
To sit with it inside of you like an anchor,
The ranchor of death,
Retracing the miscalculation of my steps,
Attempting to justify my lies.
To feel the pain I caused inside, now mine.
To understand the letter,
My angry manifesto.
For Ms. Monica,
I should have done so much better.

Stay Human

2 Save the World

I remember when I knew you.
Back then, your smile was bright,
Eyes were still white.
I knew you when your energy was so electric it magnified my life.
I loved you back then, but I knew nothing of life.
So, the sights and sounds of the street are what we'd cling to through the nights.
Innocence, lost over and again, and so,
We became angry, trying to cover up our pain.
Love, how I miss your smile,
Your confidence and wit,
The way you used to squeeze my hand when you held it.
And, whatever happened to, "Head, forever up; eyes, forever open!"?
It seems that when I went away, you got stuck out here in this thing alone, smoking dope to cope, thinking perhaps, hope's a joke.
The choices chose, landed you out there on that track, where we both know, you die slow.
My thought process seems to me selfish now.
I wish upon a star as it streaks across the midnight sky,
Mummified inside this flesh, occupied by my illusions.
My confusions contort as they rumble about inside of me,
And still, I have humble hopes of the day you return to self,
To God,
To me.
Seems odd what life has manifested.
The test, I guess, is time itself.
For now, I'll sit alone, sifting through old photos in this motel room,
Flipping through a life that seems so separate from the present,
Merely snapshots of what passed me by.
And life just is, it need not provide an alibi, yet still, I wonder . . .
How far have I wandered?
As I'm wondering to myself and blaming myself, I cry, and realize
The snapshots of a young Queen with so much unrealized potential lost in a cocaine daze, asleep,
I think . . .
The purity of past waters has ineffectively turned to slime
Or perhaps those waters were always poison?
Unenlightened, I sit frozen in thought,

June Barefield

Angry,
Frightened,
Afraid.
Any attempts to turn back, at this point, would be a return to a lifetime of crime.
Time after time, in my mind, I contemplate this end.
I cannot go backwards again.
I don't want to die, locked away in the confines, prescribed for me at the Federal Pen
Nevertheless . . .
I contact some old Komrades of mine, and
My questions are like gunfire. I can see it in their eyes.
I hit 'em with the "who" and the "what," then the "when," until the "why."
They all seem to be repulsed at your existence, laughing in that fake sort of way, charging
It all to the game,
All of it
As if your life means less today than it did yesterday.
My initial impulse is, of course, anger!
It rises up clear to my throat,
And just then, a still sort of resolve calms me.
My demons, now running away in defeat,
And when I next speak,
I speak of life and of love and of loss,
I speak of the crisis and the **K**ross,
Feeling so twisted and torn, knowing I cannot save the entire world,
Thinking, I'd remember when I knew you . . .
Knowing, I would die 2 save yours.
For Missy

Stay Human

ID

My identity was prepackaged
So was my daddy's
And his before him
At different levels
For different reasons
In different times

Taught to separate
Through the
Predetermined integration hustle
To hate
Ravaged and damaged
Never in alignment with grace
Not really . . .
Too focused on misery
Even with all the imagination and the pleasantries
So, when we lose we run
When it hurts, we wine
Disconnected from hope
Wrapped up in ego hegemony
Unaware of the soul
Chasing the almighty dollar bill down every road
Roads I do not own
Do not wish to own
Sold the message of an institutional negro that has his own **k**ross to bare
Told to worship and uphold this negro here
An institutional negro
The all ameri**K**an type
For comparison
Given this Willie Lynch-narrative
Taught to tremble in the face of the boss man
Told to go to college and gain the wisdom to understand
Standing underneath this man since the very day I adopted this evil plan
Plotting . . . my plan a direct
Indication, indicating that my education was just a scam
For control
To keep me exactly where I am

June Barefield

Chasing the almighty dollar down every road
Never told that, that Roman Road, sadly is a creation to own my mind body & soul
Now I know . . .

My identity was prepackaged
So was my daddy's
And his before him
At different levels
For different reasons
In different times.

Stay Human

The First Virtue

Politeness

The poorest, most superficial

Pure form and ceremony, mostly

What them call "etiquette"

Morality, absent

Politeness, a show

Necessary as clothes

As valuable to the Nazi

As your poot-butt preacher &

His dress rehearsal b4 the show!

Unexposed & polite

Smiling face and bright eyes

That dance together in a phony light

Them all know

THE 1st VIRTUE:

"Always B polite."

June Barefield

The World

The world is a liar, and i am the world's to devour.
It's just set up that way, like all the dope from Nicaragua.
But still,
Around here, the power of love lies between one's heart and one's nuts!
To suffer this disillusionment is just confusing shit, sure to destroy the youth in their
Innocence.
Look around.
And even now,
To live through all the fake stares and the phony smiles, dealing with the dilemma of a
Life without "life,"
Wrapped up in useless rhetoric,
Like becoming that pawn-broker with the itchy palms after they've turned your heat off in
December.
Every member of society down here, with me on main street,
Where the comparison narrative is fierce; so, we all feel forced to compete,
Accepting as truth, the messages of clowns,
Upside-down in a darkness we perceive to be light,
Paralyzed by fright we'll never admit
Until insight becomes paradise and we hunker down and commit.
At some point, a man must take the time to stop and analyze, compare and reflect on the
Neglect and disrespect for himself, projected onto others.
At some point, the only reality is the one that cannot be seen or heard, but felt,
To be possessed inside graceful corridors of a see-through deja vu, and realize that the
Legislator of these rules lives inside, where there are whole rivers of light.
Or?
Make the choice, but make it knowingly, and remain outside amongst the parasites, in
    survival mode, jockeying for a position amongst the dead, insisting that this is life,
    insisting that they're alive, attempting always to impose their might,
Blinded by the spectacle and the pretty lights,
Blind to the facts while being aware of the same,
A cruel plight, because
Sight without vision has no eyes.
To be in touch with joy and the stimuli, creating the expansion, exploding, enabling one to
    levitate in the skies
Mind's eYe, Alive!
Inside, there are worlds that we can create within our minds,
Merely reflections of the refracted passages, redacted to be re-written within,
A message for correction, corrected,

Stay Human

Calm contemplations, concerning a reconnection with love and joy, and hope and peace.
Personally, I know that I do not deserve this peace.
All I've ever given this earth is war, but
"Deserve's" got nothing to do with it.
So, I don't have any survivor's guilt, not anymore.
You see, I've been just about everywhere, done just about everything.
At this juncture, it seems, I've done it all for nothing, except for this one thing . . .
There's always been this little compass inside of me, guiding me up and over every obstacle placed in my path, unknowingly.
You see?
The wrath of my hate and hostility, this agility, just leaps
But this agility does not belong to me, not really.
Thinking back now,
Even the forlorn of prison could not undo this magnetic majesty of a particular course, plotted for only me.
Unaware, I've been just like a little penguin on his trek, waddling thru' the mess, from crevice to cliff, down through the valley and back up over the ridge
In the world, desperately searching for a purpose.
On purpose, I separate these days.
Sometimes I can't forget; so, I remember what it is that life is.
I contemplate very deeply.
I meditate until I can again think clearly.
A peace and calm returns to my world.
Contrarily, the World is lawless and violent.
It's explosive and never quite silent.
It's in the air, the climate,
Up where the ultra grandiose exploit the mindless.
In my life, most prevalent inside the stone forests of our city streets, lying horizontally, in blindness
And in capital cities across the nation where your "rights" are being bartered by the spineless.
The entire world is like one gigantic cold sore bleeding pus and blood and violence,
And for what?
If the world is a liar, what exactly does that make us?

June Barefield

On Purpose

I purposely separate myself from society at times
Escape this city bullshit
Journey to the country
A peaceful retrieve
A recovery of sorts
Of self
Attempt to write of green trees and leaves as they leave
A reprieve
And in my desperation, clumsily, I weave false tails of trails that lead me into, and then
    back out of delight
Take a deep breath and
I gaze upon a starlit night
They don't shine in the Metropolis anymore
Out in the distance, in my mind
I can hear gunfire out on the avenue somewhere
This violence consumes my life
My mind is wrapped too tight
I wonder who died tonight
Unwind must I
On purpose.
I write of simple, unconfused things
The sunlight as it falls off of a hill and then disappears
I speak to my dogs
They understand
My need to separate
To be free
To unleash something beautiful inside of me
Something beautiful has got to exist inside of me
His tail wags, and she licks my face
Unconfused for the moment
Focused on the crickets as they call out
On purpose
I escape, pulling my collar up around the nape of my neck
Pitch my tent and lay still as I relent
And I cry
On purpose.

Stay Human

"The time has come, God knows, for us to examine ourselves, but we can only do this if we are willing to free ourselves of the myth of America and try to find out what is really happening here."

James Arthur Baldwin (1924-1987)

African-American writer and civil rights activist

Comparably

From the bright Red of libido
Into the pure violet of divine charity
What is life, if not faith and hope and love
The evolution and journey into presence and clarity
A sacred geometry
Alchemy simplified?
Comparably, how does it even matter, but for the tide that flows in the affairs, and the fortunes of men?
So, to those who "believe," it seems, no evidence is necessary
The absence of Faith and Hope and Love
Ambitions
Arbitrary continuance
The preponderance of evidence is ever more relevant
Every impetus disintegrated slow
All alone together, wandering in the dark, marveling at the marvel of existence
Gathering up things, believing
But to those who disbelieve, no evidence is sufficient
Comparably, **who gives a fuck!**

Stay Human

Human ChiKens!

A Peasant competition
Inside this digital cage
Information, the age
Where the entire world population meekly participates
Enslaved to the bar code, cell phone, monstrosity of consumerism
Bought by the parents to be sold to the children
HUMAN CHIKENS!
Inflicted, infected with the virus of a conformity existence
    Compliance IS tradition
The government IS god
STATISM RELIGION
Bought by the parents to be sold to the children
Wilful ignorance, the imprint for all the "citizens"
Watched, inspected, spied upon, directed, law-driven, numbered, regulated, enrolled, indoctrinated, preached at, controlled, checked, estimated, valued, censored & tracked
Commanded by beings who have neither the right, nor the wisdom, nor the virtue to do so
"CITIZEN-SHIP"
Where the usual useful idiot and fifth columnists, now augmented by automated bots, cyborgs and human trolls are busily engineering public opinion
The autocratic civil servant villain, stoking up outrage, sowing doubt, and chipping away at trust in our institutions
But fuck the institutions, never trusted an institution
Human Chikens!
And now, it is our brains that are being hacked
   . . . ***Redact that***

Hate Speech

Fuck a government
The Republican
Democrat
The Congress
Senate
And all the executors of the oligarchs will
Fuck the bureaucrat employed by these criminals to institutionalize whatever The State sees fit to mandate
Fuck 'em!
Die slow!
Fuck the IRS
The USDA
The AMA
The NIH
The FDA
The SEC
Fuck the WHO
Fuck the Gavi alliance
The Tavistock Institute
The Trilateral Commission
Bilderberg
The CFR
Fuck the CDC!

Fuck the Autocrat and
His call for obedient slaves called citizens
Fuck 'em!

Fuck the Narrative!
The mainstream news Hunger Game Managers
As a matter of fact: Fuck you, if you believe them, wake up, chump!

Fuck Bill Gates
Elon Musk
Jeff Bazos
Larry Ellison
You know what?
Fuck the Pope and Catholicism!

Stay Human

BAYER-MONSANTO
Fuck Warren Buffett
Mark Zuckerberg
Larry Page
Peter Thiel

The Sackler family
Walton family
George Soros
The Rothschilds
Clintons
Barry Obama
Kissenger
Fuck the Rockefellers!
Die Slow!
I hate them all
Fuck 'em!
Vanguard
Statestreet
Palantir
Blackrock
Darpa
Black water
And every single comfortable black nigga perpetrating the fraud
Fuck all y'all!!
Think Louder Now!

"We have come to be one of the worst ruled, one of the most completely controlled and dominated governments in the civilized world-No government by free opinion, no longer a government by conviction and the vote of the majority, but a government by the opinion and the duress of small groups of dominant men." ~ Woodrow Wilson

Fuck Woodrow too!

June Barefield

The Falcon

The animal heads of ancient Gods are returning
I see them when eYe dream
And I don't dream much
Not these days
But more importantly
I've heard from the messenger of the unseen
"Why do you sit here so hopelessly sober? Rise, take up the cup from the falcon's beak and drink"
Across every night and the falling of the sun
In such a world as this
Wasting strength in self-denial
The bluebird and the cardinal, both mourn for the dawn
In such a world as this
Until anger alone fills up the void
Dominance, a subliminal meter
Even fear made cosmetic with plastic smiles
Measured out in unnaturalness
Sawing off every telescope with logic
For unreasonable reasons
For greed
Drawing lines for fences
Building walls for borders
Across every night, and the falling of the sun
. . . but still
I wonder if those little flowers on the cactus' aroma are sweet
If beneath mankind's feet lies an immeasurable abyss
I don't dream much anymore
Not these days
But the animal heads of ancient Gods are returning.

Babylon

Men and women "seem" to come together like vultures, dropping down out of the sky on a pretentious cloud, "believing" death is life

Love is the lie, mined by culture

And what is culture but the lust of the eye?

Every solace of being compromised for the flesh,

Searching for some magical antidote outside oneself

Into delusional realms,

Excluding ourselves,

Dropping down out of the sky,

Like vultures

. . . in love?

June Barefield

Her Eyes

Please excuse me when I no longer answer your eyes

Mine, a slight reprove, with very few denials

Another friendship we chide

Hearts never quite one, but remain full of life

You, I let teach, while I learn the "US" in we

Let you rule what concerns you have for this world as patiently as I can B

I have this dreamer's dream about life, but wishes do not define one's destiny

Silly me!

I find nothing pious or profane about the sham of this thing, frivolous as it may be

I must soon find meaning, or again, I must flee to be free

So, please

Please excuse me when I no longer answer your eyes

They lie.

Promise

It all begins normally with promises

Unhealthy expectations, excuses, excusing mere confusion

Lamentations

And then more promises

Preceded by "I'm sorry"'s

Followed by intense makeup sex

Cycles repeat and habits are formed

Unhealthy habits

A wall is painfully erected slow

Delusion grows

Love exposed

Or lack thereof

But normally, all of it begins passionately with a kiss

And a promise.

June Barefield

United We Stand

"In order we form a more perfect union"
Rid ourselves of these physiological confusions
These emotion minus devotion type fusions
Them treasonous muses that come to steal, kill, and destroy unity in unison
Like a sleeping GIANT underneath the tranquilizing sun
ONE by one
Them come
Dropping out of the sky to form alibi together
But to weather the storms of life?
NEVER.
For a time, them lie in pleasure, pleasing one another
Smothered promises underneath stained sheets and pipe dreams
Then fly apart like
Them never professed a love
Agitated by what it took
Complicated the simple
With the tranquility of a D.C. crook
Took a love that them proposed, hosed it down and killed the rose
I suppose it's all just relative
Surmise it mostly speculative
This interjection
A perception of this forever-looming Love-question
United we stand
But will you stand through it all?
I'm guessing no, so
DIVIDED we FALL.

Stay Human

Every Star

I want all the women
And all the monies
All the fun
Lots of mystery
And mayhem
One of them, wide body, buckets with plenty of legroom
So your girlfriend's real comfortable when she suck it
Fuck it!
I want a nuclear arsenal,
The governments got one!
I've gotta be able to bust back when them people come
I want a personalized introductional path to "God"
A death list
& Transparent skin
I want every single rainbow
All the stars
I want to dance out on Jupiter
Blow a little smoke when I dip down past Mars
I want all the fuckin' marbles
Every ace, king, queen, jack
A Jeanie in sexy pink panties to hold my marbles in her mutha fucking bottle
I DON'T TRUST BANKS!
I want one of them ugly cats with no fur
More room to explore
My life may indeed B a blur
But NEVER a bore
I want every star
All the marbles
Everything entire
I have nothing
But fuck it!
I will never negotiate
Ever.

Tell me tho', what's in your wallet?

June Barefield

Dreamy Enough

Sometimes while chasing my tail, dreaming about a dream, but not quite dreamy enough for me, it seems, I forget to breathe
Held my breath once for an entire week!
I just want everything right now, is all
So, when I finally inhale again, I get a little wobbly about the knees
I realize these things I want aren't dreamy enough for me!
Sit back and I think of better dreams to dream
I hear the birds again
Smell the flowers, and I wonder very deeply about me . . .
I can see the trees, but I forget sometimes to thank God for the shade underneath
To simply relax and enjoy a sunrise, and just take in a morning time breeze
Maybe spend more time in prayer and meditation to **B-peAce**
Nope.
Not dreamy enough for me!
So, I suffocate myself with me
Arms numb
Legs heavy, but I run
Shadow-boxing with a conundrum
Fighting myself about what I think I need
Where next I wish to go
My next step
Move
What path to take
I anticipate
Expect
But I don't know?
I just dream
I start to trust in everything but love, and even my imagination begins to suppose
So, while I opine inside the valley of dried-up bones and inept clones, children still smile at me as they walk by
Eyes, like sunflowers
The drumbeat that is my pulse races, but e**Y**e manage to dream a dream for them too!
I smile back, remembering small graces, like gentle rain showers, my mother's garden, and the beautiful flowers she loved so much
Hard faces, they pass me by as well, and everytime, I simply hold their gaze
I've come to realize that they're just holding their breath too! Sometimes for whatever reason these hard faces, they manage a smile too
They do!

Stay Human

That's just about dreamy enough to do whatever I think I need to, in pursuit of something
I'm unclear about, but not really
Confused?
Me too!
But I dream on . . .

Twilight approaches, but I am blind to the sky
Holding my breath up the avenue of time
Shadow-boxing a conundrum, daydreaming
About a dream I can't quite see
Numb
I forget to breathe
Dying slowly inside
Never conceding defeat
Asking why, and cursing what, back in this space again, not giving a fuck!
They think, I must comply
My city street's alibi the question
So, I testify w/o answers
Suffocating myself with me
Living out this life
Dreaming
Forgetting to breathe.

Random thought:
Before was was was, was was is.
Fucked me up too!
Not dreamy enough.

June Barefield

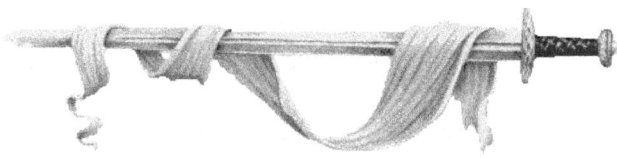

"Class struggle defines most of human history. Marx got this right. The sooner we realize that we are locked in deadly warfare with our ruling, corporate elite, the sooner we will realize that these elites must be overthrown."

Christopher Lynn Hedges (b. 1956)

American journalist, author, commentator, and Presbyterian minister

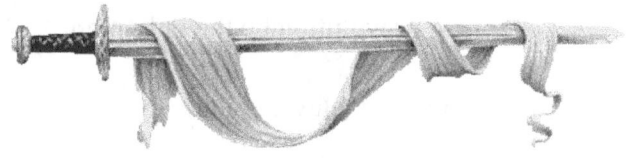

Stay Human

Anarchy Now

All books, everywhere. Free.

Bring out a postage stamp of General George Jackson, another of the honorable Mr. Leonard Peltier.

Arrest the NSA, and leave the Taliban the fuck B.

Discontinue The Monsanto Protection Act.

Find Barry Obama and kick his poot-butt ass.

Define defiance, plant a garden.

Stockpile weapons, ammunition, water, and fuel.

But NO INTERVIEWS! Fuck the media! Turn that bullshit off!

Burn all ameri**K**an history books that currently exist as institutional curriculum.

Introduce to the people "The *People's* History of these United Snakes."

Remove all black children from the ameri**K**an assimilation asylum them call school, a pipeline straight to prison.

Teach them the knowledge of themselves.

Organize, protest, riot, disobey, STRIKE, conspire together.

All people, let revolution be the only plan.

Smack a televangelist!

NOW MEDITATE.

June Barefield

Now, Here We All Are

The earth currently is a human farm where thought itself is **manufactured** for the human being; therefore, **consent** is as well. Collectively, we are all Pavlov's dog, chained together on Plato's wall. In a language older than words, the populations of people here on earth, especially in the west, are properly bewitched. The same disparaging psychology that promotes bogus science, fear-based religion, and allopathic "medicine" is programming our every assumption. We are, all of us, under a spell, clutching desperately to a world created by our captors, and we expect to be rescued by the same entity that has enslaved us. Our collective expectations themselves, crippling. But who are these people, the captors, are they even human?

If your eyes are open, then these are very strange times. We are out of sync with The Mother, Earth, arrogantly believing that She needs for us to save her! The herd is being culled right out in the open too, in plain sight, and the human condition is slavery. The human condition is ignorance. The human condition is pomposity and contempt. Whatever comes next will fall right in line with exactly what came before, more violence, and more war. Our so-called leaders all know this. Violence never begets calm; only more violence. Here, in the West, the citizenry is trained to believe that the rest of the world hates us because of our "freedoms," for our civilizational superiority, and we all believe that the rest of the world is simply barbarians.

We think that because we are ameri**k**ans that the rest of the world is beneath us. Thus, the role of the western establishment is to cry victim time after time for the atrocities we ourselves have created all over the world on a centuries-old civilizing mission. We here in ameri**K**a capitulate, I believe, because we are comfortable enough. However, if you've been only partially awake during the last decade here in our fair ameri**K**a, then you should have the sense that this "comfort" we've been afforded is coming to an end. In life, if one wishes to rid oneself of arrogance and ignorance, he or she should try poverty. From now until 2030, the captors will be diligently at work, bringing us all into a new order for the ages. All of these things have been written down, and must come to pass. I propose that the politicians the voting populace pretends to "elect" every four years are nothing more than very bad actors. The Entertainment Arm of *THE MILITARY INDUSTRIAL COMPLEX*, if you will, because war is constant. War is the one thing that these political actors always agree on. The rest of it is just a show.

In ameri**K**a, the food is poison, the skies are being sprayed with chemicals, they control the weather, our waterways are deliberately polluted, and the very soil that grows our food is being systematically depleted. In ameri**K**a, there's a process, a system of structured methodology in place, where the more organized the power elite become, the fewer non-conforming factors can be admitted. Today, more than two decades after the crafty implementation of The Patriots Act; from that moment forward, until now, the people live under constant surveillance. Your car, television, appliances, and certainly your telecommunication devices are being listened to and watched and tracked, tracing everything all of the time. Anyone applauding history and our so-called freedoms here in ameri**K**a are really just fooling themselves. The histories of mankind are histories only of the higher classes. A very effective tool history is, written by the higher classes for the sole purpose of control over the masses. Whatever the case, we who reside here together in our fair ameri**K**a are indeed witnessing the end of an era. There's a darkness perceived as light, descending upon every tribe of the human family in this world. Here, in the West, most remain under the clever conditioning that tells the citizen that anyone with any influence at all who may question authority will be considered a "conspiracy theorist," and subsequently silenced.

To question authority, especially on topics concerning Israel, or anything to do with The State Department and foreign policy is painted as deplorable. The masses of the people capitulate and comply, fearful and inept, under the masterfully controlled media machine, believing whatever they're told. It is so when "they" threaten to mark us with invisible tattoos to ID the vaccinated. When "they" tell us that we will not be able to buy or sell or participate in the economy until we have this proof of "immunity." The human species is merely some sort of cruel experiment, the entire experience.

So here we all are, 2025. The year of the digital ID. The year of the CBDC. The year of the Great Reset. The year of the COVID-19 Scam Treaty. The year of the next Great War. The year of the Deep Fake Selection, newly inaugurated, presidential actor, swearing in ceremony. The year of the Polycrisis. Here we all are, 2025, gazing out collectively over the horizons of life at pestilence, famine, destruction, and death. The masses of the people (the peasant class) are kept in the pen by jackbooted sheepdogs of the police state, led along by political puppets who "act" as their shepherds. The shepherds, meaning the politicians, the scientists, the so-called educators and intellectuals, the doctors, and of course, the lawyers and judges. Each institution that we're raised up to respect and give reverence to has been co-opted, and captured.

The fact is that the "peasant class" simply cannot afford them. Everything is under some sort of a strange hypnosis, in a trance that we have been trained to call "life," and in this place, nothing is sacred. Back in 2001, during his inaugural address to the nation, little George W. Bush proclaimed that "there is an angel, a dark angel, riding inside of the whirlwind in complete control of the storm." After lil George completed his portion of the criminality assigned for him to act upon, we went on with the fantastical "Change you can believe in"-scene, staged with extravagance and grace, to the "Make ameri**K**a great again" performance, to being told that we are "building back better," while the entire nation is suffering, and witnessing together a total dismantling of everything from small business to housing to education to basic human dignity.

What remains ever steadfast is war, and the same dark angel inside the whirlwind still controls the storm. And the people are still but peasants. The people still watch, follow, consume, and believe. Now, I am merely a peasant myself; so, I'm not asking that you believe anything that I have to say either way. What I do propose is that you doubt everything, and think for yourself. My hope is that your mind is squeezed, laid out, and dried of the MK Ultra puss called "normalization" or "progress" or yes, "democracy." The process of this systematic rendering, this "democracy," is a festering wound that only the people can heal collectively. From one peasant to another, I offer you permission through reasoning to see yourself differently. I suggest to you the question, "Who are you?" It is the answer that begs the question, "How does enigma experience time?" And so, to this question, the conditioned western mind must cognitively change its perception of humanity.

    So here we all are, 2025. Are you going to remain a captive? After all, we're all only human, but not without real freedom. Not without dignity.

Rules for Being Human

1. You will receive a body.

2. You will learn lessons.

3. There are no mistakes, only lessons.

4. A lesson will be repeated until it is learned.

5. Learning lessons does not end.

6. 'There' is no better than 'here'.

7. Others are merely mirrors of you.

8. What you make of your life is up to you.

9. Life is exactly what you think it is.

10. Your answers lie inside of you.

11. You will forget all of this.

12. You can remember it whenever you want.

Stay Human

Constantly shifting this ephemeral landscape
The natural process of the rock, waves, wood, the bone and sinew
Sometimes suddenly something is made new,
Shaping all the faces in a mist of evanescence
A crystalline snowflake shift
Delicate along distant shores, delightfully wrapped in the intricate
Again subtly shifting, always changing
Constantly evolving, advancing, rearranging, becoming human
To be
A Human Being

The simplest purification, inside heart strings
Silent strings
The pure stream
A holy incorruptible ring
A heavenly journey taken by earthbound beings
Instinct & intuition
The wilderness & her wisdom
Simple things
Silent strings
The pure stream, fixed on some mysterious cue from the superlative,
Then passed down
This life-giving grail and singular beauty,
Spectacular,
Its radiance fueled and retooled for the marathon ahead
Over and again the unbegun begin
Endurance, uncanny, lacking all but indomitable spirit and agility
Forever evolving inevitably
Call it the migrants' cleverly orchestrated connectivity to "being"
To be
A Human Being

Herein exists this naive, brilliant benevolence
A starry night sings an ever mysterious interplay
The ever illusive, all inclusive, interpolation of the life game,
Strumming heavenly heartstrings urgently slow
And ages go by

Stay Human

Time secretly and serenely engulfs more time
What is time?
In more time still
A third eYe
Connected cosmically, to be purified 7even times on this journey earthbound
And sometimes
Suddenly,
Something is made new,
Shaping the faces while the mist escapes,
Evolving into truth
The truth of becoming, to "being"
To be
A Human Being.

Epilogue

A Few Words from the Author

I don't like biographies. At least not my own. I've written some other stuff, been alive, seen some things, and done some things . . .

Genuinely, I feel as if I really, in all honesty, I haven't done shit! Compared to other people's bios, my "accomplishments" are minimal. I don't like resumes either. After all, little George Bush became president! The people in the United States considered the Harris broad for the office of the Presidency too. Not really "the people," tho, huh?

I feel like biographies are often dishonest. Not always, but often. If I were to write out an honest account of my life, I'd need to make it into a book and sell it along with mirrors to the blind in the cities across America! Perhaps turn it into a Hollywood production, have the late great John Singleton raised from the dead to create and direct it! When I say, I feel like I haven't done shit, I mean in the world of squares. I mean that respectfully too. I wish I'd lived a square's life, because the truth of the matter is that the square individual, when he or she has faith, rounds out quite nicely. Most of the "friends" whom I grew up with are dead or incarcerated. I'm here still, and it baffles me. I am very grateful to be alive and of sound mind. Lots of people might question the sound mind part, but here I B. Alive and thriving, feeling sometimes that I don't deserve to be. I've grown to realize that 'deserves' got absolutely nothing to do with it.

OK. Okay. OK.

Here we go: I was born in the heat of the summer months, something like a June bug. I spent 10 years in military service to our fair America. I traveled the world with guns, legally. I was an Airborne Ranger, INFANTRY. I was so confused in my youth that I was very proud of that. I spent another 10 years driving an 18-wheeler, crisscrossing the country. I enjoyed that. I am a very proud father of three very tenacious, revolutionary thinking children. I believe that they are my reason, my greatest accomplishment in life, and I love them all with all that I am. With my last breath I will think of them. They are my reason.

I've gone through many processes in this life. Today, I consider myself to be an anarchist. I don't 'think' like the average citizen, God bless them. Experience, environment, and training have taught me many things that cannot simply be juxtaposed with the irony of life as it is.

I raise dogs. Read. Write. I used to play chess! I pound my bony lil chest, and today . . . I try not to hide away the miraculous. Life is good. Oh, I like a good portion of Rice and Beans from time to time as well. By the way, I'm also starting a garden this year!

The Author's Afterword

Everything is thought. For a man to believe what he thinks to be true, within the recesses of his own heart and inside his own mind, is the same for everyone.

For all, what's inside becomes also what is outside, and it is our **thinking** that makes it so. Our first thought is to be rendered back upon us at the blaring of the last trumpets, in the moment of Final Judgment. The eye through which I see God is the same eye through which God sees me. The very essence of existence itself being the source from which all things emerge. But what is God? Ever present, yet we cannot discern the sum and substance of our very being. The world we inhabit is a place of twisted duality, multiplicity, illusion, and division created from thought. Chaos is the reason for the designation and establishment of the PERSON, outlined to keep The Human Animal in competition from our initial step until our last breath, divided. To hold humanity on the plane of effect, forever in reaction mode, responding and ignoring the causation of our collective plight.

We believe what is temporary to be steadfast and permanent, what is fleeting to be meaningful: We "believe" that what is false is real, and **it is thinking that makes it so**. We fool ourselves because of a lack of consciousness and care. There's not enough evidence to be found hidden away secretly in vaults at the Vatican in Rome to convince The Idiot. In every generation, there are men of means, too often from the same bloodlines, who puff themselves up on the improvement of society, but not a single individual man improves. The civilized, these men of means; they've constructed a great eyeball in the sky and ignored the power of the sun, disregarded the reasons that we are here, who we are, and what constitutes the ashes in the dust and the dirt we will return to.

Today, the masses of people live more by virtue of what the system does FOR them or TO them than by virtue of what they do for themselves. There are two distinctly separate moralities in the world. One's for the Rulers, the other for the ruled. Without knowing, I learned that shit there in public schools. We humans have been manipulated and mind-controlled into "believing," so our very senses deceive us. The life we have been gifted and then guilted into is built around appearances and the imagery that has been formulated to define for us what humanity is. Personally, I have many, many lessons yet to learn, but as of right now, **I think** at a certain level; they call it "class." We've all been purposefully misled. We've been reigned over, dominated, and commanded by a very dastardly clan for the ordering of the soul. Disconnecting reason, spirit, desire, bravery, fortitude, and courage; until all that remains for the so-called commoner, the citizen, civilian, Everyman, pleb, is just an invocation to eat, drink, and make merry in a state of captivity and panic, yearning to be governed.

We've forgotten to remember that we must live in accordance with nature. We must! Instead, we are hidden away inside these asphalt jungle carousels tied to a chain of reason, drowning in this insipid, common identity. And for us city folk, this is natural. Seemingly, the natural condition of The Human Being in this state is to be born, have a bunch of stuff happen to him, and die without control over anything at all. The attention of the human being has successfully been spooked into a disturbing state of pooled dementia and subjugation. As I look around inside of myself in the world, I am chastened by the lack of meaningful intention and callous behavior. Oftentimes, our words are coated with elegance, lacking any sincerity at all, so every action becomes burdensome; our sense of awareness is a ridiculous mime. It's time we begin to burrow underneath the soft white underbelly of our so-called culture and confront the truth about who we are, what we believe, and how we act.

Underneath all of the noise, beyond the distorted credence of belief, and behind the veil of the never-ending distraction in this material world, a place of pure naked awareness exists inside. To recognize this presence, this unchanged, profound, limitless energy is to come into, shall we say, the curiosity of Oneself. **To know Thyself** is to wake up from the spell cast upon you concerning limitations; to transcend suffering and the cycle of ultimate decay, and this idea that we've been born into concerning death. We are not separate from this essence. What I speak of is not philosophy, but truth waiting to be realized. To shatter the illusions of what we've been told, taught, directed, and authorized to "believe." *Humanity* has forgotten how to breathe, **think,** and be. We are, the entire lot of the human family, but actors. Actors who are, for the most part, totally unaware of this fact. Otherwise, we would not survive as our True Human Animal Selves in this allegedly Civilized World. Not without the disguise of persona.

The word "person" is rooted in the Latin and means "character" or "mask." None of us are real, and we think that we are. According to our personhood, our personalities, and ego, we've been cast together into life's tragic masquerade where the truth has been intentionally replicated and silenced, until even the silence is a lie, duplicated and made true enough to be relatively credible. With the knowledge of this, I ask myself, "What is real? Who am I? How can I reach through the surface levels of the finite and **Be** peace?" Knowing there's a wellness inside that the mind pollution of this world is trying to complicate, a source beyond time and space that is transcendent in every human being that they wish to dim down in dumbness, to silence by fear, and finally suffocate right up until the curtain call is made for the end of life, and the BoogeyMan Death speaks! Inside this space is breath and life, and deeper still, there is breath inside of breath, a sacred place.

As Saint Kabir poetically proclaims, "Inside the tiniest house of time, where breath rests . . ." In the last, shall we say, 15 to 20 years, I have discovered simplicity, breath control, meditation, and peace. Contrariwise, for the majority of my life, I've placed the importance of status and things, as the opinions of others, foremost in my thinking, coveting everything, all of which were outside myself. None of which ever had any real, true value. Today, I wish to covet only my breath. Breath is the bridge that connects every life to consciousness and unites the body to this *natural* process called **thought**.

Before any words were spoken or any *civilized* interpretation was given, there was only breath. No distraction or separation, just this simple rhythm of inhale and exhale; all aligned perfectly with the Natural and in sync with the earth, moon, stars, sun, river, sea, and sky. The truth is that the further we remove ourselves from what we are, and the more dependent we become on technology, the further removed from the simplicity of "being" we've become. Some would argue, less "Human." There is good reason to believe that Original man suffered from less stress and frustration and was better satisfied with his way of life than modern man is. He was certainly more in tune with Nature, and was capable of recognizing, appreciating, and respecting it with an understanding of his place in it. Not everybody is prepared for the truth or even cares to align themselves with said truth. Most avoid it for comfort and pleasure and a sense of security. Look around; everywhere is but an endless variation of sameness in countless forms. All of it seems real enough. We've got a name and a past and an identity and this belief that within the countless variations of utter sameness, we think we're different, somehow separate from one another. Language, Religion, Race, "God" & Government are all tools of division, all constructs of man, all hoisted upon this "human" creature, creating the schism.

I have been dabbling in the science of etymology for a time now because words are important to me. I was once on trial for my life and was forced to really take a close look at the language. Ever since then, my desire to define words has been an ongoing venture that has allowed me to take a peek behind the curtain and realize that the other side of darkness is merely the modeling of perception. Language is a critically essential tool used on the populace for the management and control of the people who inhabit it. There's a distinct pathology for the rich and another for the poor that includes the dumbing down of language and the control of speech. A huge part of creating useful enough "humans" is to propagate the institutionalization of the language to subdue the freedom, the actual meaning of speech as it pertains to language. To enslave the mind makes the enslavement of the physical body completely unnecessary, and language has made dull slaves out of useful men. For decades, centuries; I'd dare say, human beings have capitulated in order to attain a level of comfort and, shall we say, happiness?

We measure success with material wealth and garner whatever self-worth we possess by competing with one another, sacrificing our wellness for systems that exploit us for money. Participation in this system, where the social engineering of the "human being" materializes, has always existed. The comfort and happiness we seek are an illusion. The illusion that keeps us all complacent enough to be easily controlled. Today, the mechanisms of control are everywhere. It's in the news that keeps the people in fear, in the mindless entertainment that numbs critical thinking, in the "social norms" that reward conformity while punishing authenticity, ultimately reducing The Human Being to the status of nothing more than a domestic animal. Go ahead, say "Moo!" This is what **they** think of us all: Human cattle.

I initially thought that the title of this book, "Stay Human" was clever, caring, and carrying along with it a message, a meaning, and a purpose. NOW, I think that, given the language, maybe the title is simply bad advice. At least as far as "the language" is concerned, in reference to defining the real meaning and getting just a wee glimpse into the minds of those responsible for its creation. Initially, my thinking in reference to the word "human" was common. They depend on that. That we all think ordinary, predictable thoughts is typical. So, initially, before defining the word to interpret its true meaning, I believed that the controlling class of **humans**, the inappropriately named elite, was merely being cruel and inhumane by instituting all of the trickery, war, mass murders, racism, the superior race ideology, and all the other countless crimes committed against humanity. I also thought that there was some good to be found amongst this upper-class caste of, dare I say, humans? I can see much more clearly NOW. Through the eyes of the controlling class, what's believed about the majority of the "human" population is that we all are just breathing in and taking up space and life. Stay Human for just a moment longer, please, and follow along . . .

To be or not to be a human being?

In Ballentine's Law Dictionary, 1948 Edition, 'Human Being' is defined as follows: See *monster* in the same dictionary; monster is defined as a human being by birth, but in some part resembling a lower animal. This is an unusual definition, and like all law dictionaries on this subject, a non-definition. Again, in the Oxford New English Dictionary of 1901, 'human' is defined as belonging to or relating to man as distinguished from God or superhuman beings; pertaining to the sphere or faculties of man (with implications of limitation or inferiority); mundane, secular, (often opposed to the divine). Still human?

I have always believed that being human is something that every walk of life shares. Rich, poor, black, white, fat, skinny, tall, short, whatever . . . Together, at least humanity was ours; this is what I had in mind when titling this work. I was all wrong. It was my **thinking**, or lack thereof, that made it so. Those who control the Law, Government, the Language that makes the Law, and whose meanings are always changing, depending on the aim of those wielding this law, this language upon us all, are the driving force behind competition, status, and human identity. The enemy. Every supposed effort for progress in scientific, political, religious, and economic so-called liberty emanates from the minority, the ruling, controlling class. And their thinking is NOT our thinking. Our thinking has been formulated by these despicable *Elites*. They think themselves **gods,** while the masses lag behind, handicapped by a truth grown false with age.

Humanity is controlled in large part by fear, plugged into the collective narrative, playing a role without even realizing it, afraid of rejection and failure. Fear is the perfect tool for control. Fear keeps the human beings working jobs we can't stand, buying shit we don't need, and seeking the approval of people who do not care. Being incarnated into the meat puppet game here on earth and properly inculcated into the confusion of living, in my opinion, is not life, but something else. The dark energies in the world fomenting hate, fear, and division are the same ones that write and define language one way for themselves, while the masses of the people's understanding are completely beneath their own. They own and hold The Master Key.

The most unpardonable sin in a sick society is independence of thought. They know this. Today, as ever, the few who dare to pursue this independence of thought are misunderstood; they're hounded, imprisoned, tortured, and killed. Initially, when titling this book 'Stay Human,' I thought like many think, that humanity was our collective similarity and source of change, care, and hope. I believed it, but I was wrong. According to the very definition of the word "human," I was wrong! I think it wise to try to understand the just indignation that has accumulated throughout the entirety of the collective **human soul,** whether or not this human soul has elevated into a space of awareness or not. Knots untie and locks get picked! So, this burning, surging, ascending passion that is obviously rising in us all is what will make the storm that shapes the future inevitable.

The world that's been built around us was all constructed out of the insensitive comprehension and the cruelty of the mortal ego for control. Everything that the human family has perceived is but a surface phenomenon. Many, if not most, of society's rules are arbitrary. Time itself is a concept we've been duped into agreeing with. Money is merely paper that we've been forced to assign value to; it has absolutely zero value. Borders are imaginary lines drawn on maps by minds trapped in this human illusion. Our very sense of who we are has been shaped by external labels. Nationality, career, relationships, position, none of it is inherently real at all. It's all part of this game made up for the Human, that, collectively, we've agreed to play. To be somehow revived from the slumber of human indifference will NOT free anyone from the game; sadly, it only brings you into awareness of it.

In my personal experience, this awareness can sometimes be overwhelming. Naturally, there's a disconnect from persons who remain trapped inside the illusion because you're still bound by its rules. You've still got to pay your bills, interact with the dead, and navigate all of the systems, the institutions that you no longer believe in. This awakening period in a human soul can lead one down the path to nihilism very easily. I do not have any answers for the current condition of the collective Human Family. I only know that our participation in this version of life, completely made for us to play the role of sheep, is our greatest downfall. What I do realize in all of this "humanity" is that by the ruling class, there will be no mercy. The struggle now, in my eyes, is merely a brand new compromise. Necessity knows no law. Do not be alarmed when the starving hordes are at your door demanding bread to eat. In 2025, there is no higher heaven available to man than the one that the senses can conjure. Every generation that passes grows worse. We're effectively destroying ourselves in violence masquerading as love. To know what love does, maybe we should redefine what love is, what humanity is, and live. Really live, or perhaps, just, Stay Human.

Acknowledgements

Thank You:

Dr. Hülya Yılmaz for your patience, your expertise, and your professionalism. This book did not happen without you. I am very grateful. Thank you.

William S. Peters, Sr.: For your reserve and your steady, contagious confidence, thank you, Sir!

Special Thanks:

thecorbettreport.com
The Master Key Society
Whitney Webb
Dr. Andrew Kaufman
Dr. Bobby Price
Mark Passio
Mwalimu Baruti (The Black Awakening Movement)
Ken O'Keefe
Truthstream Media
Academy of Ideas
Kaleb Cortez Barefield
Angel Elizabeth Barefield
Ms. Laniya White
Mr. Kevin Mackey
Mr. Jeurray Ivory
Mr. Ronald Phillips

Remembering:

Ms. Janet Perkins Caldwell
Brother Shareef Abdul Rasheed
Young Sonny Costa
Ms. Angela Suntoucher Peterson
Mr. Charles SaeBe Banks
Mr. William Campbell
Mr. Michael "Bambi' Smalls
Robert James Rudolph
Ms. Monica Lewis
Young Karlos
Bonn
Mr. and Mrs. Robert and Elizabeth Barefield
Mr. Devin Duffy
Mrs. Willa Mae Washington
Mr. Robert Washington
Ms. Diane Phiffer

Glossary Notes

Natural Law: Universal, non-man-made, binding, and immutable conditions that govern the consequences of behavior. Natural Law is a body of Universal Spiritual Laws that act as the governing dynamics of consciousness.

Human **Belief** is completely irrelevant when it comes to the existence and operation of **Natural Law,** just as it is irrelevant in relation to any of the other **Laws of Nature,** such as **Gravity, Inertia, Momentum, Thermodynamics,** or **Electromagnetism.** The workings of Natural Law require NOT belief. Human Belief is irrelevant.

The Seven Laws of Nature:

1. The Law of Attraction and Vibration
2. The Law of Polarity
3. The Law of Rhythm
4. The Law of Relativity
5. The Law of Cause and Effect
6. The Law of Gender and Gestation
7. The Law of Perpetual Transmutation of Energy

Law of Freedom:

As morality increases, freedom increases. As morality declines, so does freedom. Freedom and morality are directly proportional; inversely proportional is the level of tyranny and slavery in a society as morality decreases.

Truth:

Truth is NOT based on the perceptions of human beings. Truth is objective. Simply put, truth is that which **IS.** It is that which has occurred in the past and that which is occurring presently. **That Which Is.**

Anarchy:

From the Greek prefix [an]- without, the absence of, and the Greek noun [archon]- master or ruler

Anarchy does NOT mean the absence of rules! Literally, anarchy means **No Masters, No Rulers**.

The term *"Anarchy"* is a humble term. It means **"without rulers."** It **does not** mean kidnap a banker, smack a televangelist, or blow things up and sow disorder. Anarchism is an apolitical philosophy that champions the individual and decries the monarch. Anarchy is the triumphant concept that people should live unobstructed by laws and rulers but instead be consumed with the self-determination that enables kindness and care, love, and hope.

Sovereign:

Derived from the Latin adverb [super]- above, and the Latin noun [regnum]- rulership; control, or one who is above the Rulership or Control of another. Simply put: **NOT a subject or a slave.**

Authority:

Authority is the illusion created and born out of mind control, based entirely on violence. Authority has been developed upon the erroneous and dogmatic BELIEF that some people are Masters with the moral right to command others. According to Authority, others are slaves who are morally obligated to **OBEY** the Authority of the Controllers, their Masters.

Definition:

A statement of the exact meaning of a word. An exact statement or description of the nature, scope, or meaning of something.

The more accurate our DEFINITIONS for words or concepts are, the better our **clarity** of meaning, and therefore, our UNDERSTANDING of those words or concepts will be.

Man's Law:

Based upon dogmatic BELIEFS (constructs of **mind**), complied with due to **fear** of punishment, differs by location based upon the whim of **legislators** (Moral Relativism), changes with time based on the whim of legislators **(Moral Relativism).**

Government:

From the Latin verb gubernare - "To control," and the Latin noun mens - "mind." **Mind Control.**

Plutocracy:

A country/government run and controlled by the wealthy minority.

Religion:

From the Latin verb *[religare]* - To tie back, to hold back, to thwart forward progress, to bind.

Religion is a system of control, based on unchallenged, dogmatic BELIEF, which holds back the progress of awareness and consciousness.

Solipsism:

From the Latin adjective solus - "alone," and the Latin pronoun ipse - "self." An ideology that says that only one's mind is sure to exist. Solipsists contend that knowledge that is outside of one's own thinking is unsure. That there is No Such Thing as OBJECTIVE TRUTH; that there's nothing of the external world and its workings that can ever actually be KNOWN.

References

The Ucc Connection

Robson, David. *How to Free Yourself from Legal Tyranny*

The Limits to Growth. A Club of Rome project on the predicament of mankind

Bukowski, Charles. *War All the Time*

The Three Initiates. *The Kybalion: Hermetic Philosophy*

C.S. Lewis. *The Magician's Twin*

A Big History of Globalization: The Emergence of a Global World System (World Systems Evolution and Global Futures)

Guevara, Ernesto 'Che'. *Guerilla Warfare*

Keith, Jim. *Mass Control: Engineering Human Consciousness*

Spangler, David. *Towards a Planetary Vision*

Mullins, Eustace. *The Curse of Canaan: A Demonology of History*

Jung, C. G. *The Undiscovered Self*

References contd....

Smith, Adam. *The Invisible Hand*

Camus, Albert. Resistance, Rebellion, and Death

Other Books

by the

Author

The Author's Works
Can Be Found at

www.innerchildpress.com/june-barefield

Or in Other Fine Book Outlets

BANG!

&

GET IT OVER WITH!

98 PERCENTILES

June Barefield

Inner Child Press

Inner Child Press is a publishing company founded and operated by writers. Our personal publishing experiences provide us with an intimate understanding of the sometimes-daunting challenges writers, new and seasoned, may face in the business of publishing and marketing their creative "Written Work".

For more information:

Inner Child Press

www.innerchildpress.com

intouch@innerchildpress.com

Inner Child Press International

'building bridges of cultural understanding'

202 Wiltree Court, State College, Pennsylvania 16801

www.ingramcontent.com/pod-product-compliance
Lightning Source LLC
Chambersburg PA
CBHW081935170426
43202CB00018B/2928